The Great Fire
at Hampton Court

The Great Fire
at Hampton Court

Michael Fishlock

with drawings by the author

Foreword by
HRH The Prince of Wales

The Herbert Press

Copyright © 1992 Michael Fishlock
Copyright under the Berne Convention

First published in Great Britain 1992 by
The Herbert Press Ltd, 46 Northchurch Road, London N1 4EJ

House editor: Julia MacKenzie
Designed by Pauline Harrison

Set in Sabon
Printed and bound in Great Britain by
BAS Printers Limited, Over Wallop, Hants

A CIP catalogue record for this book is available
from the British Library.

ISBN 1-871569-49-4

Frontispiece: Hampton Court Palace, 31 March 1986 (Rex Features)
Front cover: Fountain Court, 31 March 1986 (London Fire Brigade)

Contents

Acknowledgements 8

Foreword *by HRH The Prince of Wales* 9

1 Fire! 11

2 Taking Stock 22

3 Rescue Begins 34

4 Salvage and Discovery 46

5 Survey and Planning 59

6 Craftsmen and Contractors 68

7 Restoration Begins 76

8 The Carvers 85

9 Topping Out 99

10 Handover 115

Appendices

I The Salvage Squad 122

II The Working Party 122

III Principal Consultants 124

IV NADFAS Volunteers 124

V Donors 125

VI Species of Fungus and Shells 125

Index 127

For Carole

Acknowledgements

This account of the fire is not an architectural treatise but the story of the events of the fire and the people who worked together to restore the Palace to its former glory.

I would also like to dedicate it to Longley's workmen, who produced results of outstanding quality, to the Apartment 49 design team, and to the public who supported us throughout.

Thanks are due to many colleagues in the PSA, Hampton Court Palace and James Longley and Co. for information, advice and encouragement; in particular, Jim Brooks, Glyn George, Daphne Ford, Crawford Macdonald and Liz Trebilco.

The photographs on pages 6–7 and 24–5 are reproduced by kind permission of Hampton Court Palace. All other Crown Copyright photographs are reproduced courtesy of the PSA Photographic Branch and the Historic Royal Palaces Agency. All Longley photographs were taken by Barry Kemp Photography.

Thanks also to Francesca Sayers and Gill Sims who did the initial typing, and to my son Mark for his long hours of objective criticism and editing.

I am grateful to Julia MacKenzie for her patient help with the text and to David Herbert for his confidence in taking on an 'unknown'.

Especial thanks are due to Max Arthur and to my son John, without whose persistent urging this book might never have been written.

Note

Imperial measurements have been used throughout.

Following the reopening of the restored apartments, the First Presence Chamber is referred to as the Presence Chamber, the Second Presence Chamber as the King's Eating Room, and the Audience Chamber as the King's Privy Chamber. The former names have been used in this book.

(previous page) Aerial view of Hampton Court Palace before the fire (Crown Copyright)

KENSINGTON PALACE

The fire which broke out at Hampton Court on Easter Monday, 1986, devastated much of the south range of Fountain Court. It filled all who knew the Palace with sadness and dismay.

I remember visiting the still smoking ruins of Sir Christopher Wren's fine building on the day of the fire and looking at the blackened and water-soaked rooms. They were filled with rubble and stood open to the sky where roof and floors had collapsed in the intense heat.

Even while the fire was still burning, volunteers had managed to carry out to safety nearly all the works of art and within hours teams of architects, engineers, conservators and craftsmen had begun the salvage and rescue of the building itself. They set out to save the hundreds of fragments of carvings, mouldings and panelling from the debris and to sift through the ashes to recover crystals from the magnificent Audience Chamber chandelier. Their success made it possible to incorporate much of Wren's original fabric into the restored building.

Although a terrible tragedy, the fire provided an opportunity to unearth long buried knowledge of the original structure and to reinstate many features of Wren's original design. In the process, fascinating mementos from the past have been revealed, including hidden messages from eighteenth century workmen and mysterious handprints on plastered walls. This book tells the story of painstaking recovery and restoration which made all this possible.

Charles

1 · *Fire!*

1986 was the year of Halley's Comet. Appearing approximately every seventy-six years, this comet has traditionally been associated with disasters: it appeared in 1066, for example, the year William the Conqueror defeated King Harold at the Battle of Hastings, and in 1910, which was when King Edward VII died. Its passage in 1986 was to prove no exception.

Early in the morning of Easter Monday, 31 March 1986, I arrived back in London from a holiday in the USA, where I had seen Halley's Comet brilliant in the black sky over the Arizona desert. My route home from Heathrow airport goes past the imposing form of Hampton Court Palace. The distinctive decorated red-brick chimneys are its trademark, as instantly recognizable as the dome of St Paul's Cathedral or Nelson's Column in Trafalgar Square. That day, however, the skyline did not have its familiar form. Billowing clouds of smoke swirled high above the chimneys of the Palace, their undersides glowing orange from the reflection of the flames coming from the building.

Red-and-silver fire engines lined the main drive to the Palace, their warning lights winking. A damaged hose leaked a steady stream of water into the gutters. Cars and curious members of the public were gathered at the iron entrance gates, and it took some time to get clearance to go inside. As an architect working for the PSA (Property Services Agency) with special responsibility for Hampton Court Palace, I was allowed through.

Stepping over more hoses, I made my way towards Fountain Court, where the fire was concentrated. I walked through cold and empty courtyards echoing with the shouts of firemen, all very different from the familiar warm atmosphere created by the mellow brickwork I knew so well. It was hard to believe that fire was tearing the heart out of this peaceful place.

As I entered the cloister of Fountain Court, the reality of the situation became clear. On the opposite side of the courtyard, great flames were raging on the top floor and smoke poured through the partly collapsed roof. To my right, a fireman was perched precariously on top of a long ladder, directing a jet of water through the blazing windows. On the grass by the fountain, other firemen were struggling to connect a second hose.

Early salvage work after the fire (David Utting)

I watched as sections of the third (top) floor collapsed, sending tons of burning timber and lead into the Cartoon Gallery below. As the debris hit the floor, a dense cloud of dust and smoke was forced out of the first-floor windows and floated back up the face of the building.

By 9 a.m. the entire top floor was ablaze and flames were leaping high above the roof. The hose on the grass suddenly surged into action and a fierce jet of water hit the face of the building, splintering fragments of stone from the window surrounds and dislodging slabs of cill and cornice. As the high-pressure jet found its target through the open windows, the roaring sound of the fire turned to a hiss and clouds of steam mixed with the black smoke.

Gradually the flames above the roof began to subside and the orange glare from inside the building grew fainter. Pieces of burning timber continued to fall through the building, landing in showers of sparks on the floors below. The fire brigade declared the fire 'surrounded' at 9.40 a.m. The quick response of the emergency services to the initial alarm – the first two appliances arriving from Twickenham Fire Station within six minutes of the call – prevented the fire from spreading to the adjoining sides of Fountain Court and a greater disaster was successfully avoided.

Fighting the fire from the South Terrace (The Guardian)

At about 9.30 a.m. a group of us had made our way inside the building, through the King's Guard Chamber and on towards the Cartoon Gallery. The Cartoon Gallery is the largest of the King's State Apartments, and had been designed by Sir Christopher Wren to house the Raphael Cartoons bought by Charles I in 1632. In 1865 the Cartoons were transferred to the Victoria and Albert Museum, and were replaced by seventeenth-century Brussels Tapestries Good fortune, or, perhaps, a more benevolent comet than Halley's, had saved these tapestries from damage. They had been removed for cleaning and although due to be returned, had not been rehung at the time of the fire.

The scene in the Gallery, was one of utter desolation. Black slime covered the floor, water streamed down the panelling and dripped like black rain from the gaping ceilings above. Smoking debris was piled high and a charred beam from the collapsed ceiling stood almost vertical, like a javelin embedded in the floor. In the gloom, pieces of rubble suddenly burst into flame and then subsided, hissing, under the jets of water. The scene was an extraordinary mixture of sights, sounds and smells. The overall impression, however, was dominated by water – underfoot, overhead, and cascading down the walls.

Gerald Drayton and his team from the PSA Works Office had been making

Firemen in the Second Presence Chamber (Colin Pain)

holes in the floors since the early morning to let water drain through to ground
level. This was essential to prevent the whole of the first floor from collapsing
under the enormous weight of water. Gerald made one of the saddest comments
of the day when he said: 'We spend all our lives maintaining and caring for
this building, and now I'm smashing holes in it in order to save it.'

We climbed to the eastern end of the top floor. 'They're still looking for
Lady Gale', we were told. Lady Gale was one of the elderly residents of the
Palace's grace-and-favour apartments. All the other residents had been led to
safety and she was the only one unaccounted for. Although it was too early
to be certain, it seemed likely that the fire had started in her apartment and
spread throughout the top floor, before breaking into the rooms below.

We went into Mrs Bailey's apartment, which adjoined Lady Gale's. Thick,
greasy soot covered every surface and when I moved a bowl, its white shape
stood out on the blackened formica worktop. Then a bizarre thing happened.
A telephone rang. I found the phone and picked up the receiver. It was one

of Mrs Bailey's friends who had heard news of the fire on the radio and was calling to check that she was safe. It was a surreal experience to stand in the middle of the chaos and confusion holding a normal telephone conversation.

Downstairs the invaluable work of the Palace Salvage Squad (see Appendix I) was being discussed. The team had gone into the building within minutes of the alarm being raised. With the floors and ceilings in constant danger of collapse, they had carried to safety nearly all the pictures, furniture, ceramics and tapestries from the State Apartments.

The full extent of their achievement became apparent later, when it was discovered that of all the irreplaceable treasures in the apartments at the time of the fire, only one painting had been destroyed. A total of eighty-four pictures, some very large, had been carried to safety through thick smoke, as well as fifty pieces of furniture, seventy ceramic items, two large tapestries, two carpets, two chandeliers and many other small works of art. The squad was aided by

Knocking a hole to let water drain away (Colin Pain)

(left) The Audience Chamber, 2 April (Jim Brooks); (right) HRH The Prince of Wales visiting the Palace, 31 March (Rex Features); (below) The burnt-out roof on 2 April (Jim Brooks); (opposite) The Cartoon Gallery, 31 March (David Utting)

some firemen when rescuing two of the largest paintings from the Cartoon Gallery: *The Embarkation of Henry VIII from Dunkirk* and *The Family of Henry VIII*, both from the school of Holbein.

Nonetheless, the squad did have one disappointment. Access to the smouldering building was strictly controlled by the fire brigade and its fears about the imminent collapse of the ceiling in the Audience Chamber meant the salvage squad failed in their attempts to remove the great crystal chandelier. However, as we shall see, the story of the chandelier did have a happy ending.

The Salvage Squad is led by Joe Cowell, Superintendent of the Royal Collection, and trains once a month in the techniques of handling works of art in emergency situations. On the day of the fire the team of eleven included a joiner, a foreman, two gardeners, a stone mason, a storeman, the verger of the Chapel Royal, and three of Joe's sons.

By mid morning the rooms at first floor (Principal) level had become scenes of great activity. Juliet West and John Thorneycroft of English Heritage (the government-funded conservation body with responsibility for the built heritage) were assessing salvage possibilities, while trying to discourage firemen from throwing debris out of the windows. In normal circumstances this is a perfectly legitimate part of fire-fighting, but in the case of an historic monument such as Hampton Court, the rescue and salvage of all material, however badly damaged, is of major importance to any later restoration.

Jenny Band and Graham Goode of the Crown Suppliers Textile Studios (now the Textile Conservation Studios of the Historic Royal Palaces Agency) were dragging pieces of throne canopy from the black rubble and immersing them in baths of de-ionized water for cleaning. As they recovered piece after piece of sooty fringe, their spirits rose; they were amazed how much material had survived.

In addition, among all the paraphernalia of fire-fighting, salvage and emergency repair, television camera crews and reporters milled around, seeking interviews wherever they could. And in the afternoon, after I had left, concerned distinguished visitors arrived. HM The Queen, HRH The Prince of Wales and HRH The Princess Margaret visited the Palace to see the damage for themselves. Kenneth Baker, Secretary of State for the Environment, had already been, together with other ministers and the local MP, Toby Jessel. Meanwhile, Sir Oliver Millar, Surveyor of the Queen's Pictures, had already begun conservation work on some of the rescued paintings.

When I returned later in the afternoon, the scene was calmer than when I had left. The fire engines, ladders and hoses were gone, and the journalists had departed. The building stood bleak and melancholy, the walls still dripping with water. And in my absence a body had been found, which was later identified as that of Lady Gale.

I walked past the rubble in the Cartoon Gallery and went up to the third floor. Below me a lone fireman, there to ensure no smouldering debris flared up again, stood among the piles of brick, timber and broken fragments of furniture. During the morning, amid all the smoke and chaos, there had been little time to think of repair. But now, beginning to understand the extent of the damage, and realizing that tragic as the fire had been much of the fabric of the building remained, I began to think of restoration. But where to start?

As an architect, I had, like Gerald Drayton, been helping to maintain the Palace for a number of years. However, this fire had left problems far beyond the capacity of our relatively small maintenance group. Historians, conservators, security and fire advisors, quantity surveyors, architects, builders, palace administrators, tapestry and painting specialists would all have to work closely together to ensure that no one group delayed or inhibited the work of another. But we could be sure that all would be motivated by a profound desire to see the Palace restored to its former beauty.

As I walked back through the desolate apartments, the afternoon light had almost faded. I stopped to pick up a charred fragment of card lying in the rubble. It read, 'Lady Gale requests the pleasure of the company of . . . . . RSVP'. It was a poignant end to a sad day.

Hampton Court Palace in 1740 (Cliff Birtchnell)

2 · Taking Stock

Hampton Court has been a royal palace since 1529, when Cardinal Wolsey gave his sumptuous home to Henry VIII in a vain attempt to win back lost favour.

Situated beside the river Thames, fourteen miles upstream from London, Hampton Court has been a favourite of British monarchs ever since, although George II (1683–1760) was the last to use it as a residence. Queen Victoria opened the Palace to the public in 1837, and it is now one of England's most popular historic buildings; in 1986, the year of the fire, there were 605,000 visitors.

William and Mary, who came to the throne in 1689, were particularly attracted to Hampton Court, not least because its rural location provided a welcome relief for the King, who suffered from asthma and was grateful for the means of escape from the polluted London air.

The old Tudor buildings were too dark and draughty for late-seventeenth-century taste, however, and the Surveyor General to the King's Works, Sir Christopher Wren, was commissioned to design a new, modern palace. The splendour of Louis XIV's palace at Versailles had captivated all of Europe, and Wren's brief was to build a worthy rival. His original design involved the demolition of almost all the original Tudor buildings, leaving only Henry's Great Hall. It is perhaps fortunate that Wren's grand design was never fully realized.

Christopher Wren's initials over a door in Fountain Court (Cliff Birtchnell)

Plan of Hampton Court Palace

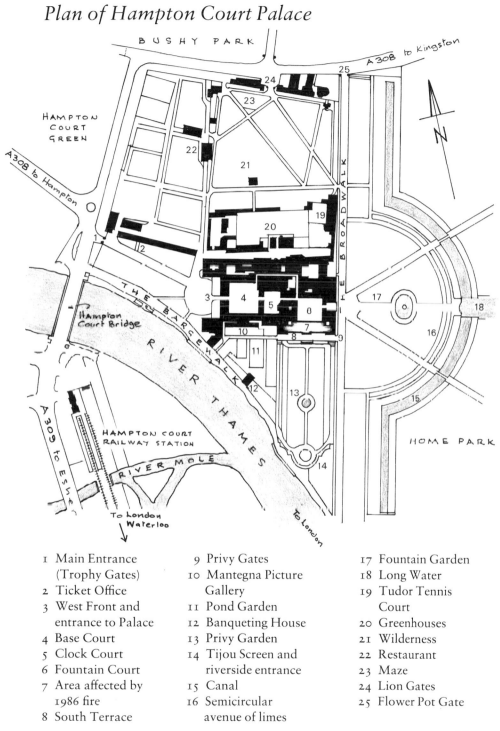

1 Main Entrance (Trophy Gates)
2 Ticket Office
3 West Front and entrance to Palace
4 Base Court
5 Clock Court
6 Fountain Court
7 Area affected by 1986 fire
8 South Terrace
9 Privy Gates
10 Mantegna Picture Gallery
11 Pond Garden
12 Banqueting House
13 Privy Garden
14 Tijou Screen and riverside entrance
15 Canal
16 Semicircular avenue of limes
17 Fountain Garden
18 Long Water
19 Tudor Tennis Court
20 Greenhouses
21 Wilderness
22 Restaurant
23 Maze
24 Lion Gates
25 Flower Pot Gate

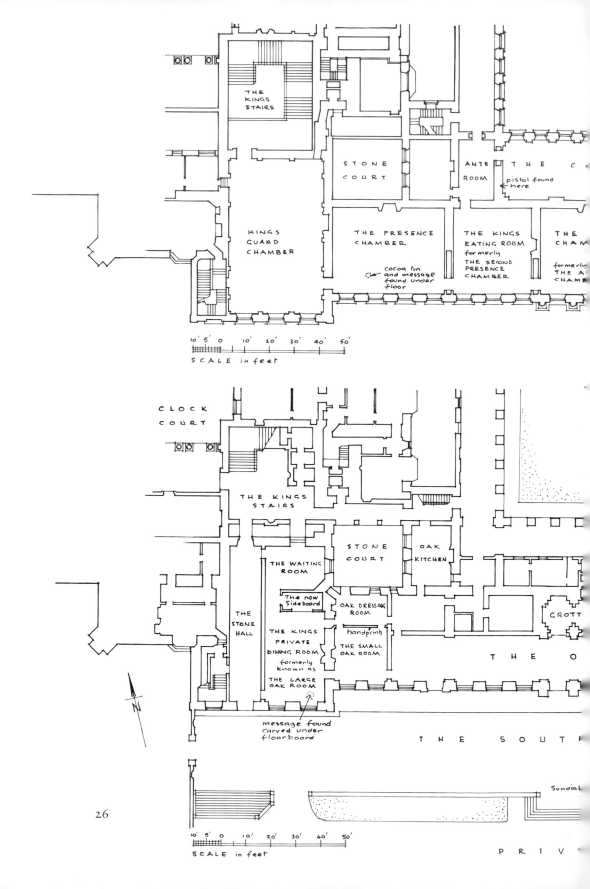

THE
KINGS
STAIRS

STONE
COURT

ANTE
ROOM
← pistol found here

THE C

KINGS
GUARD
CHAMBER

THE PRESENCE
CHAMBER

THE KINGS
EATING ROOM
formerly
THE SECOND
PRESENCE
CHAMBER

THE
CHAM

formerly
THE A
CHAME

cocoa tin
and message
found under
floor

10' 5' 0   10'   20'   30'   40'   50'

SCALE in feet

CLOCK
COURT

THE KINGS
STAIRS

STONE
COURT

OAK
KITCHEN

THE WAITING
ROOM

THE
STONE
HALL

The new
Sideboard

OAK DRESSING
ROOM

handprints

GROTT

THE KINGS
PRIVATE
DINING ROOM
formerly
known as
THE LARGE
OAK ROOM

THE SMALL
OAK ROOM

THE O

N

message found
carved under
floorboard

THE SOUT

Sundial

26

10' 5' 0   10'   20'   30'   40'   50'

SCALE in feet

PRIV

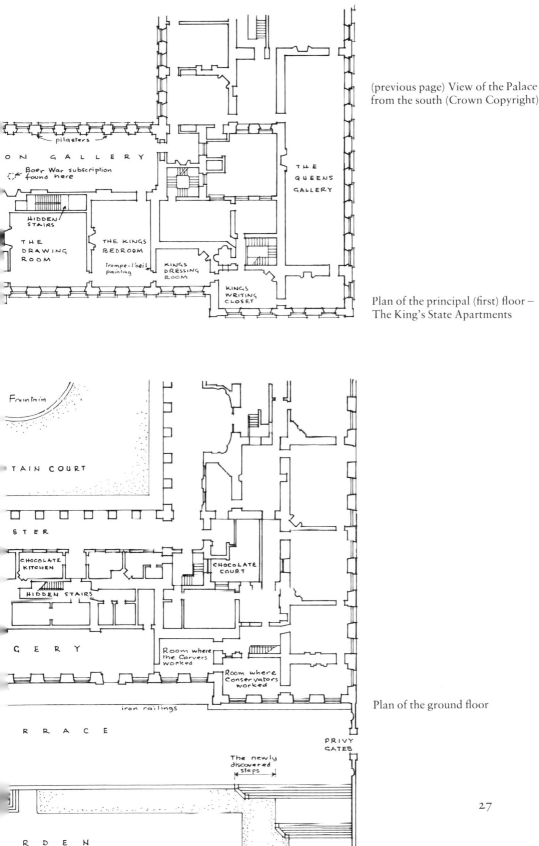

pilasters

O N G A L L E R Y

Boer War subscription found here

HIDDEN STAIRS

THE DRAWING ROOM

THE KINGS BEDROOM

trompe-l'oeil painting

KINGS DRESSING ROOM

KINGS WRITING CLOSET

T H E QUEENS GALLERY

Fountain

TAIN COURT

S T E R

CHOCOLATE KITCHEN

HIDDEN STAIRS

G E R Y

Room where the Carvers worked

Room where Conservators worked

CHOCOLATE COURT

iron railings

R R A C E

PRIVY GATES

The newly discovered steps

R D E N

(previous page) View of the Palace from the south (Crown Copyright)

Plan of the principal (first) floor – The King's State Apartments

Plan of the ground floor

27

The final scheme comprised a group of elegant baroque apartments on the site of Henry's Cloister Green Court. Built in brick and stone, it became known as Fountain Court and provided accommodation for Queen Mary to the north of the courtyard and for King William to the south. Wren skilfully integrated his design into the adjoining Tudor buildings in such a way that, from the east, the impression was created of a complete baroque palace. Internally, the rooms were decorated with the work of great contemporary artists and craftsmen: the carver Grinling Gibbons, the painter Antonio Verrio, and Jean Tijou, the ironsmith.

During the course of construction part of this wing collapsed and had to be rebuilt. Disaster was to strike again in the nineteenth century. Almost exactly one hundred years before the 1986 fire, in November 1886, forty rooms north of Chapel Court were badly damaged by a fire which was started by a naked flame and then spread through timber panelling and partitions. The *Graphic* of 27 November published the following report of the incident:

THE FIRE AT HAMPTON COURT PALACE

THE suite of rooms where the fire broke out on Friday, November 19th, had been allotted by the Queen to Miss Cuppage, but she was away at the time, and they were temporarily in the occupation of Lord Alwyne Compton. About 11 A.M. smoke was seen to be issuing from the first floor of the building, which consists of three storeys, and is situated on the north side of the Chapel Court. The flames spread rapidly, and the local appliances proved insufficient to cope with them; but after a while steamers and manuals arrived from various adjacent towns, while at 3 P.M. Captain Shaw, Chief of the Metropolitan Fire Brigade, appeared on the scene. By that time the flames had been got under control, and at 4 P.M. all except one of the engines were able to quit the premises. While the fire was at its height, the flames penetrated through the second floor to the roof, a portion of which fell in about 1 P.M. A large body of police kept the approaches to the scene clear of spectators, while some of the firemen and a detachment of the 10th Hussars performed useful work in saving the furniture and other belongings of the occupants. The firemen ran much risk, on account of falling timber, but only one person—an onlooker—was injured, and he very slightly. Miss Somerset, a bedridden lady, had to be rescued by means of the trap-door in the roof, and carried along the leads. Altogether, this was a very alarming conflagration, and the historical pictures and other art-treasures had a very narrow escape. As it was, thirty rooms were burnt out, much of the masonry will have to be rebuilt, and the damage done is estimated at 20,000*l.* It is said that a maid-servant put a mineral-oil lamp—which she believed to have burnt out, but which was really still alight—into a cupboard, and that this caused the fire.

Burnt-out rooms illustrated in the *Graphic*, 27 November 1886

Miss Somerset was rescued by a Mr Thorne, who was subsequently awarded the medal of the Humane Society.

Four years earlier, in December 1882, Mrs Lucas had not been so lucky. Her attempt to make tea over a spirit lamp was the cause of another serious fire. Her bedroom was close to the Queen's Gallery and after the panelling caught fire, she rushed out to raise the alarm. Unfortunately, she went back, possibly to collect a much-loved possession, and was later found suffocated by smoke.

The fire on that occasion was dealt with by the eighteen-man palace fire brigade, who enlisted the help of Captain Ramsay and his men from the 4th Hussars, who were quartered nearby. The repair bill was £4,000 and that for the 1886 fire was £8,000 (£186,200 and £428,240 at 1992 prices). Both incidents led to improvements in safety precautions. These included the replacement of old coke fires with hot-water central heating, and the introduction of an electric alarm system.

The similarity between the three fires became increasingly apparent as the events of Easter Monday 1986 began to unfold. Each blaze had been caused by a naked flame, and in two of the three cases, the unfortunate resident in whose apartment the fire started, lost her life. The spread of fire through timber panelling had been a significant feature and in each case the prompt action of the fire-fighting services had prevented a disaster of much greater proportions.

On the morning after the 1986 fire, Tuesday 1 April, the press coverage was extensive. The papers carried dramatic pictures of gutted rooms and saturated debris, as well as aerial shots of the smoking brick shell. Many also had a photograph of Lady Gale.

Daphne Gale was the widow of General Sir Richard Gale, who had commanded the 6th Airborne Division in the D-Day landings, was ADC (General) to The Queen 1954–7 and in the years 1958–60 was Deputy Allied Commander, Europe. His widow was seventy-five, a grace-and-favour resident and rather frail.

Grace-and-favour means exactly what it says. As a reward for their loyal service, The Queen graciously permits, at her own discretion, certain retired members of her Household or the armed services to live in apartments at her palaces. However, although it is a great privilege, the accommodation is often not as grand as one might expect. At Hampton Court, many of the apartments consist of large, draughty rooms and are situated on the upper floors. Carrying the shopping up six flights of stairs is laborious, and this has led some residents to devise an ingenious rope-and-pulley arrangement to haul their baskets up from ground level.

There was now no doubt that the fire had started in Lady Gale's bedroom. The fire brigade's investigation branch identified a spot near the external wall where they believed a flame began to smoulder in the carpet. This then burnt through into the floor space below. The depth of charring on the floor beams suggested a slow, smouldering fire. A high-temperature blaze would have resulted in severe surface scorching.

The investigation team concluded that the fire probably began shortly after midnight and continued to burn at a low level for several hours. By 5 a.m. it had reached the floor cavity above the Cartoon Gallery. At 5.20 a.m. a security alarm went off in the Palace control room and two guards were sent to investigate. They found no evidence of a break-in, but did notice that the paint on the ceiling of the Cartoon Gallery was bubbling. They called the Security Officer, Glyn George, who, realizing that the problem must be in the area above the ceiling, went immediately to the apartments on the third floor. He used a pass key to open Lady Gale's door but was driven back by thick smoke. He covered his face with wet towels and tried again, only to be forced back a second time.

By now the fire brigade had been called and Ian Gray, the Palace Superintendent, was rousing the other residents and leading them to safety. The fire brigade found that although the smoke was thick there was little heat or noise from inside the apartment. This suggests that at this stage, about 6 a.m., the fire was still contained within the panelling and floor spaces. Ten minutes later, when they made another attempt to enter Lady Gale's apartment, their progress was halted by an enormous increase in heat. The 'cold, slow-burning' fire, as it was later described in the official report, had flared up and become a raging inferno.

Flames appeared from the third-floor windows, broke through into the roof and finally engulfed the entire top floor. More assistance was called and fire engines raced to the Palace from all directions. Altogether more than 120 firemen fought the blaze.

The inquest on Lady Gale was opened on 7 April and immediately adjourned by the Queen's Coroner. It resumed on 29 May and a verdict of accidental death was recorded. In his report, the coroner, Lieutenant-Colonel George McEwan, wrote: 'I am satisfied that no one else was connected with the fire, that there was no incendiary material involved and no electrical fault. It would certainly appear from the evidence that the fire was connected with Lady Gale personally, perhaps by smoking material or by a lit candle.'

The forensic scientist who inspected the damage said: 'In my opinion the fire originated in the main bedroom between the bed and the window and was the result of the ignition of furnishing fabric or paper by a naked flame or a lit cigarette.' The exact cause of the fire will probably never be known.

The fire was of such significance that a formal investigation was necessary. The Secretary of State for the Environment appointed Sir John Garlick to 'enquire into the role of the Department of the Environment in relation to the fire at Hampton Court Palace on March 31 . . . with particular reference to:

1. Maintenance 2. Fire precautions 3. The action taken when the fire was discovered.'

The terms of reference excluded any inquiry into the cause of the fire, except in so far as it might have been the result of some act of omission on the part of one of the department's officers.

The inquiry took three and a half months and Sir John interviewed officials from all the organizations involved with the affairs of the Palace. His report, published 3 July 1986, set out a possible sequence of events leading up to the fire. It dismissed any suggestion of a conspiracy, but concluded that there had probably been a delay in the response of the fire-detection system which allowed the blaze to become more firmly established than it might otherwise have done. However, he found no evidence to suggest that this delay had any bearing on the death of Lady Gale.

Sir John made a number of important recommendations regarding fire precautions and proposed various modifications to the automatic fire-detection system throughout the Palace. The majority of these were put into immediate effect and the remainder incorporated into the restoration project.

The Great Fire at Hampton Court

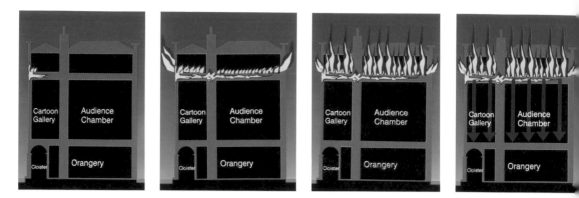

Diagrams showing how the fire progressed

The temporary roof and stairs on the South Front (Crown Copyright)

The temporary roof (Crown Copyright)

3 · Rescue Begins

The Property Services Agency (PSA) is only the latest in a line of government departments which have had the job of looking after Hampton Court since it was acquired by Henry VIII. The Office of the King's Works had the longest tenure, and the post of Surveyor General was filled by some of the country's most distinguished architects, among them Inigo Jones, William Chambers, James Wyatt and, of course, Sir Christopher Wren.

After the reorganization of the Office of the King's Works in 1832, the list of departments responsible for maintaining the Palace has an almost biblical ring to it:

The Office of the King's Works
became
The Office of Woods, Forests and Works
which became
The Office of Works
which became
The Ministry of Works
which became
The Ministry of Public Buildings and Works
which became
The Department of the Environment
which produced
The Property Services Agency

The advantage of having a special department responsible for buildings such as Hampton Court is that experienced advice is always on hand to deal with emergencies. This was demonstrated perfectly on the morning after the fire, Tuesday 1 April, when we realized that despite the drama and scale of the blaze, repair would be possible. The top floor of the south range of Fountain Court was completely gutted, and the King's Apartments severely damaged by charring, falling debris and water. The entire building was saturated and would take years to dry out.

The initial problem was to decide which of the many essential jobs should be tackled first. On 3 April the Hampton Court Working Party was set up under the chairmanship of the PSA. It had one objective: 'To co-ordinate all activities relating to immediate problems created by the fire and to plan for the restoration.'

The working party initially comprised six representatives from the PSA, two from Hampton Court Palace and two from English Heritage (see Appendix II). It met twice a week for the first month, then weekly and finally monthly until completion five and a half years later. Altogether there were 104 sessions at which all aspects of the restoration were planned and controlled. More than seventy-three experts and specialists contributed to the discussions. The co-ordination provided by the working party was largely responsible for the successful completion of the project, on time, and within the context of good conservation practice.

At the first meeting, four urgent problems were addressed: protection from the weather; structural safety; salvage; damp control.

The first of these had been tackled by Gerald Drayton on the day after the fire. He arranged a meeting at the site with the scaffolding firm SGB. He sat their representatives in his office at 10 a.m. and refused to let them leave until they had designed a roof to cover the damaged area. At 4 p.m. they emerged with a complete design, and two days later construction was underway.

Scaffolding soon enveloped the building and silver sheets of aluminium were unrolled across the roof. Clear panels were incorporated to let in light from above, and latticed horizontal beams ran through the building, bracing both the external and the central spine walls. The temporary roof was finished in eighteen days, and provided protection for the next four years. To the great credit of the engineers, it survived the big storms of 1987 and 1990, which raged across the south of England; proof indeed, that a rapid design is not necessarily a flimsy one.

Stairs were built on the north and south faces, allowing access to every level without having to pass through the undamaged parts of the Palace. It was important to isolate the area in this way so that the rest of the Palace could be re-opened to the public as soon as possible. Visitors were readmitted to most areas on 7 April, only six days after the fire, and to the rooms immediately adjoining the damaged section two weeks later.

The temporary roof was bought outright, because its cost of £112,000 worked out cheaper than the hire-charge for the four years of its anticipated use. When the rebuilding began in 1988, the ownership of the roof was transferred to the contractor, who, on dismantling it in 1990, gave the PSA a credit of £60,000 for the component parts. The deal gave the British taxpayer good value for money.

The second priority of the working party was safety. The burnt-out shell was dotted with partially supported beams and trusses. Loose material balanced precariously on ledges, while sections of ceiling swung in the draughts which

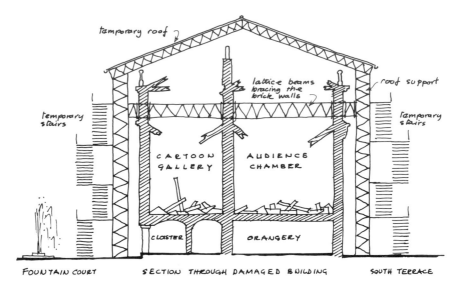

temporary roof

lattice beams bracing the brick walls

roof support

temporary stairs

temporary stairs

CARTOON GALLERY

AUDIENCE CHAMBER

CLOISTER

ORANGERY

FOUNTAIN COURT   SECTION THROUGH DAMAGED BUILDING   SOUTH TERRACE

blew through the open windows. In one room there was the strange sight of an old water boiler suspended in space, hanging by its own pipes.

It was too dangerous to work below this fragile canopy. Salvage and survey could not proceed properly until it was made safe. Engineers Cliff Nursey of the PSA and Keith Weston of English Heritage, following the working party's instructions to 'keep as much in position as possible', worked with a team of experts from the Demolition Co-Partnership Company. Their task was to lower to safety, prop up or support the dangerous structure.

There were two reasons for wanting to leave things undisturbed. First, it was important to retain as much original material as possible and second, any attempt to remove large beams and trusses might have caused further damage to the adjoining brickwork.

Some large sections of timber did have to be removed and, for ease of handling, were cut into smaller pieces. During this process the idea of reusing the charred beams began to look feasible, because the saw cuts showed that the charcoal layer was relatively thin.

Salvage, our third task, was a long, exhausting and dirty job. Periodically, there was criticism that it was taking too much time. But we were resolute that we had to keep everything. Burnt or unburnt, each piece of debris was a valuable clue; at best it might be incorporated into the repair, at worst, it would serve as a pattern for replacement. Builders, like the firemen on the first day, wanted to tidy up and had to be restrained. Tiny fragments of Grinling Gibbons carvings or scraps of moulded architraves might otherwise have ended up in the skip.

Partially de-charred roof truss (Crown Copyright)

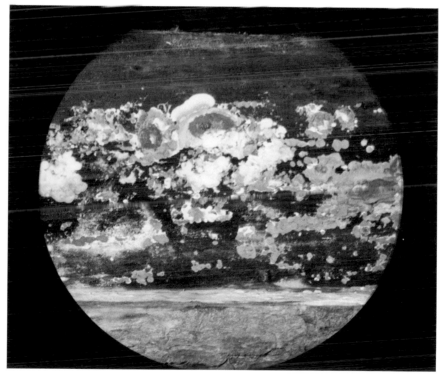

Fungus growing under the floor (Brian Ridout)

Examining salvaged items (Terry Moore)

This policy of 'total salvage' proved to be the right one, even though it took a considerable time to extricate, label and identify each fragment. In the final analysis it was calculated that 75 per cent of the original oak panelling had been reused, 62 per cent of the soft-wood panelling, 64 per cent of the original mouldings, and 9 per cent of the structural timbers. The intention was not so much to save money on new materials, as to ensure that as much of the original fabric as possible remained intact.

The drying-out process was begun within days of the fire, by the architectural firm of Hutton and Rostron. Brian Ridout of Ridout Associates then saw the job to completion. In the early days every saturated item had to be stored for drying, which did create a problem of space.

English Heritage played a major role in the early stages of the salvage operation. Daphne Ford, their recorder, became one of the most familiar figures on site. She would often appear through a hole in the floor or from behind a pile of tangled debris, dusty but smiling.

Meanwhile, the warm, damp spaces within the structure, were providing the ideal conditions for mould, fungus and, most damaging of all, dry rot. The latter is endemic in most historic buildings, lying dormant until conditions are right for its resurgence. Conditions after the fire at Hampton Court were perfect.

To make a full assessment of the situation, deep holes were drilled into the hidden voids and cavities, fibre-optic tubes inserted and photographs taken. A jungle of fungus was revealed, in which ten different species thrived, covering the moist interiors with multi-coloured mould (see Appendix VI). All this was summed up in a colourful headline in a Canadian newspaper: 'Optical fibres find underworld of fungus in famous royal digs.'

Not all fungal growth is damaging and it was important to discover where the timber-destructive fungus was concentrated and to ventilate those areas as a priority. Floorboards were taken up and debris removed, to allow cold air to be blown through the worst affected areas. Sensors were installed to monitor moisture levels as the building gradually dried out. But it was to be two years before the structure was dry enough to receive new timber.

There have been several examples of damage occurring in damp buildings where adequate time has not been allowed for the drying-out process. This has resulted in outbreaks of dry rot and the loss of much new material. The consequences have been unnecessary costs and some very unwelcome litigation.

The working party also considered how the restoration work should be documented. Correspondence and minutes would form a basic archive, but a more graphic record also seemed essential. After meetings with the BBC and various independent production companies, the PSA decided to commission the Central Office of Information (COI) to film all aspects of the salvage and restoration. The aim was to produce both a record for the archive and a documentary which could be broadcast.

Filming took place on thirty-eight days; the first on 19 April 1986 and the last on the day of the handover, 2 October 1991. This comprehensive film record includes everything from scaffold erection to picture restoring, from de-charring to re-carving. An important feature is the interviews with the many specialists, designers and advisers who have been involved with the project. For rapid retrieval, more than forty hours of footage have been carefully indexed.

A record of still photographs began on the day of the fire, and was organized by the PSA's Jim Brooks, continuing until the restoration was completed. Members of NADFAS (The National Association of Decorative and Fine Arts Societies) sorted, indexed and mounted more than 39,000 prints taken during the following five and half years. This involved over 5,000 hours of voluntary work (see Appendix IV).

Painstaking work of a different kind resulted in the rescue of the seventeenth-century chandelier from the King's Audience Chamber. This was one of the great successes of the whole project.

When Joe Cowell's Salvage Squad was ordered to leave by the fire brigade,

The COI films repairs to the Cartoon Gallery cornice (Longley)

before the ceiling collapsed, the chandelier seemed lost. We knew it must lie among the debris, but had no idea how much of its frame or how many of its crystals had survived. The English Heritage Central Excavation Unit was called in and, led by David Batchelor, carried out what was in effect an archeological dig.

Working from the edges of the room to the centre, they slowly sifted the debris until, one by one, the crystals were recovered. In the middle, the crushed frame lay in the ashes, like a corpse from Pompeii. A board was carefully eased under the frame, which was then taken to the Palace Conservation Studio for an initial dusting. Together with the hundreds of rescued crystals, it was crated and sent to Delomosne and Son of Kensington for repair. Delomosne straightened the twisted frame and began the task of washing the crystal beads to remove ash and discolouration. To everyone's astonishment and delight not a single bead had been lost.

Many had fractured when cold water hit the hot rubble and these were repaired by using an adhesive sensitive to ultra-violet rays. When the job was

(above) The frame of the chandelier uncovered (David Utting)

(below) The restored chandelier (Delomosne and Son)

finished, no evidence was left of the join. Any beads not visibly split were nevertheless tested for faults. Where these were found, the crystals were then deliberately broken and rejoined in order to prevent a hidden weakness causing problems at a later date.

The restoration took a total of 300 hours and after the crystal beads had been repaired and restrung, the chandelier hung glittering in the studio, prior to its reinstallation at the Palace. It was a breathtaking sight.

During April, the fire claimed its second victim. George Indge was the PSA fire patrolman at the Palace. He was a popular man whose duties included checking that fire extinguishers were filled, hoses well maintained and other fire fighting equipment working and in a state of readiness.

After the fire, he became convinced that he had made mistakes which had contributed to the disaster. On 5 April, he talked to Glyn George and Ian Gray and was clearly very depressed. They tried their best to reassure him, pointing out that his last day of duty was 27 March, and that the fire-detection system was known to be in working order during the first part of the Easter weekend. No action of his could possibly have affected the events of the following Monday.

On Sunday evening, 6 April, George Indge was reported missing. Glyn and Ian organized an exhaustive search of the 1,000 rooms in the Palace, as well as the cellars and garden buildings. They personally searched the roof spaces, but all to no avail. Three weeks later, on 26 April, George's body was recovered from the river at Thames Ditton. His death was as tragic as it was unnecessary, and a great loss to his family and colleagues.

The news of George's death brought a renewed surge of media interest and dramatic headlines appeared, suggesting arson as the cause of the fire in an attempt to cover up defective work.

These rumours were later rejected by the police, who described the stories as 'pure speculation'. And in his report, Sir John Garlick stated: 'During my inquiry, a tragedy occurred involving the fire patrol officer who had been employed at Hampton Court Palace. He had not been involved with the automatic system after about 6.30 p.m. on Thursday March 27. I should therefore like to say, in the interests of avoiding speculation, that whatever his actions may have been on that Thursday, I consider that they were too remote from the following Sunday night for his involvement to be regarded as material to the events connected with the fire.'

Towards the end of the month, there was yet another flurry of press speculation, prompted by two further fires. Furniture belonging to Mrs Bailey, Lady Gale's neighbour, had been badly damaged by water, and sent to the restoration workshops of A.J. Brett and Co. in north London. On 29 April a fire swept through Brett's workshops and Mrs Bailey's furniture suffered for a second time.

Thirty-six hours later there was another fire at the works. The coincidence intrigued the press, but the police could find no evidence of arson, and both fires were attributed to accidental causes.

On 26 April a more important article had appeared in the *Spectator*. It was by David Esterly, a carver in America. He described with great personal sadness the loss of the Grinling Gibbons work at Hampton Court, remarking that 'some of the most magnificent carving in the land had perished'. It was a pleasure to write to David with the news that although there was indeed a significant amount of fire damage, only one seven-foot panel had been totally destroyed. The remaining thirty had survived, although two were particularly badly charred and would need extensive repair. This was my first contact with the man who would eventually play a central role in the restoration of Gibbons's intricate work.

On 26 May, the areas of the Palace Gardens which had remained closed to the public were reopened. The damaged section of the building had been entirely enclosed and salvage work was well advanced. The emergency phase of the project had come to an end and we were ready to move forward to a period of strategic planning and practical conservation.

As the weeks passed, the architectural profession took an increasing interest in the project and began to express its views on the ethics of the restoration. Letters appeared in *The Times*; one suggested putting a glass pyramid over the burnt-out buildings and leaving the evidence of the fire on permanent exhibition. Some favoured a late-twentieth-century-style repair, using steel and plastic to rebuild the State Apartments.

Others, however, were more conservative, and when the Secretary of State confirmed the working party's recommendation that the Palace should be restored to its former glory, 'using traditional materials and construction', the principles upon which work would be based were firmly established.

(left) Handprints found in the plaster in the Small Oak Room
(Crown Copyright)

(above) Mirror awaiting conservation (Crown Copyright)

4 · Salvage and Discovery

When the oak panelling and floorboards were removed, the building shed its last protective skin. For the first time in 300 years, we were able to see the structure as Sir Christopher Wren's workmen had seen it. And we made some exciting discoveries.

On taking up the floorboards to aid ventilation, we discovered many thousands of seashells packed between the joists. Six varieties of estuary cockles were identified (see Appendix VI). It was known that Wren had used seashells in his buildings, and there is a record in the seventeenth-century accounts of barrels of shells being brought by river to Hampton Court. What we did not know was the extent of their use. It would now appear likely that Wren used them for sound insulation to prevent the noise of courtiers' footsteps from disturbing the King in his rooms below.

Wren's innovative building technique had an added bonus in 1986, because the shells slowed down the rate of burning, giving the salvage squad more time to remove furniture and works of art. However, not all the shells could be recovered from the debris. Those that were collected were put in bags and stored for future use. But the shortfall left us with a problem.

We worked out a plan with the children's television programme 'Blue Peter' for a seashell hunt for children during their summer holidays. The scheme was abandoned, however, when we realized that the hunt might produce many more shells than we needed. Accepting defeat, we decided to use mineral wool and vermiculite to fill the gaps.

The oak panelling was also removed for reasons of ventilation. Each panel was marked with a brass tag giving its location and then stored in racks for the slow drying-out process. Some panels were completely undamaged, others severely burnt; all were kept for examination and assessment.

With the panelling gone, the plaster revealed a fascinating array of drawings, signatures and graffiti. Wren's workmen, it seems, were as fond of doodling as their twentieth-century counterparts. There were elaborate signatures, matchstick men, a lighthearted drawing of a man smoking a pipe, and a particularly sensitive one of a man carrying a sack, perhaps of seashells! This last drawing is one of several which we decided to cover with glass panels. However, because it is situated on a section of wall where tapestries are now hung, viewing by the general public is not possible.

Drawing in King William's Bedroom of a man carrying a sack (Crown Copyright)

Drawing in the Second Presence Chamber of a fireplace surround (Crown Copyright)

There were other drawings, including one of a fireplace surround, executed with great confidence and clarity of line, which suggested that one of the architects or supervisors was explaining an aspect of the work to the men. It is interesting to speculate whether the sketches are an example of Wren's own hand, that of Grinling Gibbons, or maybe William Talman, Wren's Comptroller of Works.

In the King's Bedroom, there are some fine examples of *trompe-l'oeil* paintings on the plaster. These show samples of panelling and were probably made for the King's or Wren's approval. A note in the accounts of the time states that Robert Streater, Sgt Painter to the King, was paid the sum of £22 'for painting in distemper, two great rooms in the new building for patterns'. When the panelling was refixed, some sections were hinged so that visitors can now see this unusual work.

An even more powerful link with the seventeenth century was made when we discovered a group of handprints in the plaster walls of a room on the ground floor. There were seventeen individual prints pressed into the plaster, two of left hands and fifteen of right hands. Our initial thought was that they were the work of labourers 'leaving their mark', but we later found that this may have been too hasty an assumption.

The handprints were clear and well defined and photographs of them were printed in *The Times*. Within days we received a letter from an organization called The Medieval Graffiti Society, whose director later came to view the prints. She was interested, but felt the evidence was a little too modern to warrant her group's attention.

The Fingerprint Society, however, was more enthusiastic. They sent a team to Hampton Court to make a plaster cast of one of the prints and to photograph the others. Under special lighting, these photographs showed up in extraordinary detail the lines and contours of the hands.

Martin Leadbetter, the secretary of the society, confirmed that the prints were made by three different people and that they were probably men. He was also inclined to think they had been left by visitors to the Palace and not by the workmen. The society's imaginatively titled journal, *Fingerprint Whorld* (sic), carried an article about the Hampton Court prints in its July 1987 issue.

In 1991 the prints were again photographed and published as part of a routine progress report. This time, the response was even more unexpected. We received a letter from Bettina, an agony aunt/palmist, who contributes a regular feature to *Chat* magazine. Readers with emotional problems write to her, enclosing a photograph of their palm, on the basis of which she gives them advice.

Bettina saw the latest photographs and wanted to know whether she could examine the prints more closely. She came to our office and we projected the prints on to a screen, eagerly awaiting her interpretation. Her reading was as follows:

'This man could have achieved something. He could have been famous. Whoever he was, he would have been a very wealthy man, a very generous man . . . with a fantastic sense of humour. Very intelligent . . . very meticulous . . . and very clever with his hands. He got on very well with people generally. This chap shows a failing of eyesight in later years . . . he used his eyes in a lot of meticulous work.'

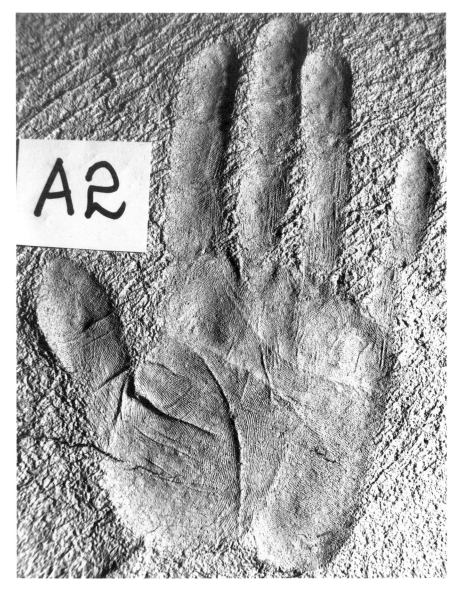

One of the handprints in the Small Oak Room (Nick Hall, Hertfordshire Constabulary)

Bettina then went on to say that she thought some of the prints belonged to the architect of the building. She claimed to know nothing about the life of Sir Christopher Wren, but despite this, her description did bear a remarkable resemblance to known facts about him.

We were all impressed, particularly when she went on to read the palms of members of the team with disturbing accuracy. It proved to be an extraordinary afternoon, with senior members of the architectural profession sitting in a darkened room, hands outstretched, having their futures told by a mysterious lady from a popular magazine. We were all hoping that the contractor's site manager would not choose that day to pay us an unexpected visit.

A few weeks later we received another letter, this time from a Mrs Ofra Livay who lives in Harley Street. She is a practitioner of 'psycho-chirology' which she described as: 'applied handreading in line with the Holtzman Method, the only discipline in psychological diagnosis to date based entirely on handreading and whose scientific validity has been established in laboratory tests.'

She too had seen photographs of the handprints, and in her analysis asserted that they were made by 'a very sensitive and highly intelligent man, who is unable to remain passive towards his environment. Early childhood traumas caused him to underestimate himself and contributed to him becoming so diffident. An idealistic and creative man . . . a very generous and human person . . . his striving for achievement is great and it is likely that he found it in academic work. He had a very original mind and a grasp of artistic values similar to Picasso. He fulfilled his potential . . . he was firm in avoiding compromise . . . applying his ideas to useful enterprise.

'If Mr A was the architect of the Palace (and this, in my opinion, is what he was), then the building and its surroundings were aesthetically planned, taking into consideration their function and not forgetting for a moment their intended purpose. In his warmth and sincerity, Mr A would have given priority to the needs of his clients and not his own glorification. Personal glory was not his aim '

The similarity between this and Bettina's reading was remarkable. From two independent and unsolicited sources, coming from both the intuitive and the scientific wings of the field, we had received almost identical analyses. In each case the finger of suspicion was pointed firmly at Sir Christopher as the perpetrator of the prints.

I wrote to Professor Kerry Downes of Reading University, Wren's biographer, in the hope that he might know of an impression of Wren's fingerprint or even an inky smudge on one of his drawings. Unfortunately for us, Wren appears to have been a meticulously clean draughtsman and, to his knowledge, no such print survives.

The Fingerprint Society was pessimistic about the chances of obtaining a readable impression by dusting any of Wren's original drawings. In any case, as the process uses potentially corrosive chemicals, it is unlikely that any curator or archivist would give us permission to try. So we will probably never know whether the prints were made by Wren, by one of the articulate and creative men in his team, or whether perhaps someone even more important than Wren himself decided to leave a mark for the future in the wet plaster.

There is one last find worth mentioning here. Behind the panelling in the Cartoon Gallery we discovered a fully loaded .32 revolver. It dated from the early 1900s but was hidden with a copy of a 1950s' magazine and the menu from a regimental dinner. It was handed to the police in whose custody it remained. Ultimately they destroyed it, but not without pulling the trigger and finding, to their surprise, that it fired first time. We wondered if the gun was perhaps evidence of some crime contemplated but never committed.

These discoveries livened up the arduous job of salvage, which occupied a great deal of time in those early months after the fire. Many irreplaceable items remained at risk and needed protection or removal to a safe place for storage. Fragile seventeenth-century mirrors, or pier glasses, for example, which had been fixed between windows in the State Apartments, had received only temporary protection after the fire. Cracked and damaged, they now needed to be carefully dismantled and crated for future restoration.

Patricia Jackson, conservation specialist in ceramics and glass, and tutor at West Dean College in Sussex, led the team which carried out this delicate work. Fractured pieces of glass were securely taped and the damage noted before packing.

The Grinling Gibbons carvings, situated high on the walls over fireplaces and doors, were particularly vulnerable to falling debris and inadvertent damage from scaffolding. The museum conservators, Plowden Smith, were brought in to dismantle carefully the carvings and lower them to the floor. Anna Plowden and Peter Smith packed tissue paper into the spaces between the intricate leaves, flowers and fruit, so that any vibration while moving the carvings would not cause further damage. The seven- and ten-foot drops were placed in narrow coffin-like boxes for storage.

It was during this part of the operation that we began to appreciate the privilege of working with Gibbons's exquisite carvings at 'bench level'. Impressive as they were high above our heads, close to they were outstanding.

In October 1986 David Esterly made his first visit to the Palace in order to see the boxed carvings. We had commissioned him to make an assessment of the damage to each piece, which could then be used as a basis for planning the repair. His list included a catalogue of missing petals, broken leaf-tips and cracked stems, as well as some thought-provoking observations about the carvings themselves.

None of the seven-foot drops was carved from a single piece of wood. Most were assembled in three sections and had two or three overlays, or superimposed layers, which built up the depth. There was clear evidence that in at least two cases, the composition of the carving had been altered. David suspected that at some time the carvings had been taken down for repair, divided into their constituent parts and then put back in the wrong order.

There was also a strong indication that two or more complete drops had been fixed in the wrong locations. Each carving, although an individual piece, had been designed as one of a pair, each a mirror image of the other. Above two of the doors, the carvings did not follow this pattern. Instead they faced in the same direction, like spoons in a cutlery drawer.

The carvings flanking pictures over the west and east doors in the Drawing Room as they were before the fire (the profiles have been exaggerated for clarity)

Had Gibbons made a mistake? Unlikely, we thought. A more plausible explanation is that workmen in the eighteenth or nineteenth century took the drops down and were less than conscientious when it came to putting them back.

A record was made of the nail holes in the back-boards as well as the nail positions on the carvings. Analysis of these, together with faint pattern marks on the backings may one day provide the answer. But meanwhile, it left us with an interesting question in relation to our overall policy of returning every-thing to its original state. Should we repeat the workmen's mistake, or seek to rehang the drops as Gibbons intended?

In addition to David Esterly, we were aided in our work on the Gibbons carvings by Trevor Ellis, who came to our notice in an unusual way.

We had been greatly encouraged by the many letters which flooded in daily from well-wishers. These ranged from an offer to make coffee, from a 'true blooded member of our English Heritage', to one from a picture restorer who said he could repaint any lost masterpiece so that it was 'indistinguishable' from the original. Many other craftsmen offered their services and cheques and dona-tions arrived from all over the world (see Appendix V). Often people just wanted to express their sadness at hearing the news of the fire.

In the summer of 1986 we decided to hold a tea party in the burnt-out shell of the Palace as a way of thanking our well-wishers.

The idea came from Charmian Lacey, who was then Superintending Architect for the Royal Palaces. She obtained the consent of the Royal Household and sent out invitations to fifty people to come for tea and sandwiches. The guests were given a guided tour of the fire-damaged area and were shown slides of how the salvage was progressing.

It was at this tea party that we first met Trevor Ellis, although in circum-stances which nearly led to his arrest. A tall gentleman was seen examining the damaged Gibbons carvings and was later observed pocketing what appeared to be a small piece of the priceless work. Tactfully, one of the working party challenged the stranger, who clearly expected to be sent to the Tower. Trevor explained that he had brought a piece of his own carving to compare it with the work of the master. It was in fact his piece and not Gibbons's which he was about to take home.

Another visitor that day was Jo Martin, a trained nurse who worked with blind and mentally-handicapped people in Brighton. She had written to us ask-ing whether she could have some of the burnt timber, having found that the tactile nature of working with rough wood was particularly beneficial to her group. We loaded her Mini with unwanted lumps of charred beam and watched as, heavily laden, she headed home. Nine months later, three ladies from the hospital came to the Palace and presented Ian Gray with a beautifully shaped and polished wooden sculpture. They asked whether it could be called *Restor-ation*. It was put on display in the Fire Damage Exhibition at Hampton Court.

(opposite above) Selecting timber for Jo Martin: (l to r) Colin Pain, Charmian Lacey, Jo Martin, John Thorneycroft (Terry Moore); (opposite below) The finished sculpture, *Restoration* (Crown Copyright)

At the same time as we were progressing with the salvage work, rebuilding work was beginning. In areas which did not involve the use of timber, and so were spared the lengthy drying-out process, building work was soon ready to start. By October, damage to the Portland stone parapets, balustrades and window surrounds had been fully assessed and the specifications for repair were finalized.

The obvious choice of contractor was Dove Brothers, who had carried out routine brick and stone repairs at the Palace for twenty-five years. Established in 1781, their speciality was repairing the twisty red-brick Tudor chimneys. In 1981 they had been awarded the Brick Development Association certificate of merit for this work. Now it was their skill in stonemasonry which was required. Using their existing contract as a basis, a satisfactory tender was prepared and on 18 November 1986, work began to repair the damaged parapets. Every stone was numbered and an assessment made of which could

Preparing stonework for repair with resin (Crown Copyright)

Dove's workman repairing the parapet (Crown Copyright)

be repaired and which needed replacing. This was recorded in detail by English Heritage.

Interesting archeological evidence began to emerge. By examining the seatings and fixings of the roof trusses in the stonework, it was possible to work out which trusses had been in their original positions at the time of the fire and which had not. This confirmed an earlier examination of the numbering of the roof trusses, which showed that four were out of sequence.

Such information added significantly to our knowledge of the building collapse which had occurred during construction of the apartments in 1689. On that occasion Sir Christopher Wren was brought before a board of inquiry set up by the King to investigate the incident. Two men had been killed and Wren found himself in a difficult position.

He managed to justify his building techniques but not without being subjected to some unpleasant and petulant criticism from William Talman. Fortunately for Wren, Queen Mary accepted some of the responsibility for the accident, acknowledging that because she had urged Wren to speed up the building work, proper supervision had become difficult.

English Heritage later found clear evidence of sub-standard mortar in the brickwork and this, together with details of the rearranged roof trusses, has enabled them to establish the precise location and cause of the collapse.

1986 drew to a close with salvage complete, contract preparation about to commence and repairs to the stonework well underway.

It ended on a particularly pleasant note. Jenny Band, Joe Cowell, Glyn George and Ian Gray were all appointed Members of the Royal Victorian Order (MVO) in the Queen's New Year's Honours List. In addition, Jesse Daniels, a member of the salvage squad and verger of the Chapel Royal, and Keith Taylor, the security guard who assisted Glyn George on the morning of the fire, each received the Royal Victorian Medal (RVM).

5 · Survey and Planning

By January 1987 an office for the PSA team had been set up on the ground floor of the Banqueting House at Hampton Court Palace. This became the 'ops room', and having a permanent base on site contributed greatly to the generally smooth progress of the project. Problems which arose in the morning could be addressed during the day and dealt with by the issue of instructions or drawings at the end of the afternoon. This ability to turn things around quickly helped win confidence from contractors, specialists and clients.

Working from the Banqueting House, with its serene riverside location, meant that not only were we privileged to be restoring one of Sir Christopher Wren's magnificent buildings, but also we were co-ordinating the work from within the confines of another. There was a pleasing sense of historical continuity, and throughout the project we felt the great architect was keeping a watchful eye on us.

The PSA design team was responsible for carrying out the structural and architectural work, while the electrical, mechanical and quantity surveying was handled by consultants (see Appendix III). A programme of work was drawn up, with the autumn of 1988 as the target for starting the main rebuilding contract. We estimated that about 900 drawings and schedules would be needed for the work to be properly described and subsequently priced. The target of 900 drawings in twenty months meant a production rate of about twelve completed drawings a week, more than two a day every day. The draughtsmen were in for a lot of late nights.

A full specification of architectural, mechanical and electrical work would also be required, as would a Bill of Quantities. This is a comprehensive list of all the materials and labour necessary to carry out the work. It is set out so that prospective contractors can price each item separately.

The previous October, the working party had organized a 'Think Tank' to explore and report on all aspects of the refurbishment. We locked ourselves away for a whole day and discussed the fundamental principles of the project, before breaking into smaller groups to analyse specific aspects of the work in greater depth.

We talked about such matters as the selection of craftsmen, how we would keep the public informed of progress, and the systems of communication which would be needed to avoid duplicated or unnecessary work. We tried to identify all the major decisions and when they would have to be made.

At the end of the day each group reported back with its conclusions. These were examined and a strategy was agreed by the full working party. The basic reconstruction and contractual policy determined that day by the 'Think Tank' remained virtually unchanged throughout the duration of the five-and-a-half year project.

The 'Think Tank' also produced a sound basis for working out the cost of the job. Earlier off-the-cuff estimates from a variety of sources had ranged from £3 million to £30 million. We now felt able to predict with some confidence a figure of £10 million, although we excluded from this the cost of picture and tapestry restoration. On the basis of this figure, together with the agreed schedule, the working party was able to proceed with contract preparation.

The survey work which had begun in 1986 continued. Engineering surveys identified the hundreds of cracks, fractures, damaged and unusable elements of the structure. Using this information, designs for new roofs and floors were drawn up and decisions taken regarding the use of burnt beams and trusses. Experiments with de-charring had shown that, to our great delight, most of the salvaged wood remained strong enough to be reused.

Photographic surveys produced prints which, after correction for distorted perspective, were reproduced to a precise scale. These are referred to as 'rectified photographs' and the process is called 'photogrammetry'. We had the option of either turning these into drawings, or writing notes and coded instructions on the photographs themselves. We decided on the latter, which proved to be a valuable timesaver.

English Heritage carried out a detailed archeological survey, which had both a practical and an academic value. Many of their drawings formed the basis for contract documents, while their investigations threw new light on Wren's construction techniques, the sequence of his building operation, and the alterations he made, or which were forced upon him by the King. For example, it was discovered that after the building collapse of 1689, additional wrought-iron floor and wall supports were put in. This might suggest that after his difficult time in front of the board of inquiry, Wren decided to play safe and introduce extra reinforcement.

In addition, the survey revealed that like many architects, Wren used the earlier building, which had been demolished, as a quarry for the new construction. Stones from Henry VIII's Cloister Green Apartments were found built into the seventeenth-century walls.

The architectural survey, meanwhile, was producing information regarding the state of panelling, joinery, flooring, walls and ceilings, while searches went on in libraries and archives for copies of Wren's original drawings for the Palace. Gradually, the building was yielding up its secrets and providing information upon which future repairs would be based.

When Wren designed the Royal Apartments for William and Mary, he also laid out the semicircular Great Fountain Garden to the east of the Palace. The famous lime trees which formed the avenue were, by the 1980s, diseased and dying. Many had already fallen and been replaced in a rather haphazard way. In 1987 the bold decision was taken by the Secretary of State to cut down the remaining trees and replant the entire avenue with new limes, according to Wren's original design.

This presented an exciting and unique opportunity. If we could use the wood from these felled limes in the reconstruction of the Palace, it would be another important and very tangible link with Wren's work in the seventeenth century. A number of twelve-foot lengths were cut from some of the best trunks and set aside for the recarving of the Grinling Gibbons drops.

However, when, two years later, the carvers finally took their chisels and cut into the white timber to fashion the intricate curves of Gibbons's flowers and fruit . . . they struck metal. What they had found was lead shot, probably the result of musketry practice or deer culling, which over the years, as the trees grew, had become deeply embedded in the trunk. It was a good idea which proved unworkable in practice. However, we were consoled by the knowledge that we had uncovered yet another link with the Palace's past.

Remaking a sliding sash (Longley)

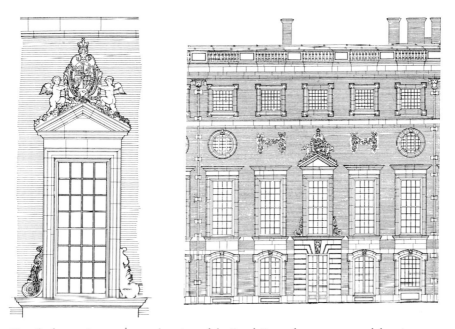

Detail of a window and part elevation of the South Front from a measured drawing by Hugh Maule FRIBA, 1896

As the first anniversary of the fire approached, media interest increased and a press conference was held to report on progress. Most of the national dailies attended and gave the project extensive coverage. BBC Radio 4 had featured the restoration in a 'Kaleidoscope' programme at New Year, and they were keen for an update.

Donations and good wishes continued to arrive and at the beginning of April two Canadian ladies came to the Palace with a cheque for £1,100. The Stratford Ontario Festival Theatre had raised the money in a raffle and the two had won the trip to England to present the cheque in person. After meeting Lord Skelmersdale at the Houses of Parliament, they arrived at Hampton Court, where we were delighted to give them a guided tour.

Dealing with visitors made great demands on everybody's time. Unfortunately, many requests had to be politely refused, although there was an equal number which had direct relevance to the job in hand. There were also the frequent VIP trips, which could not be avoided.

We had now reached possibly the most important stage in the entire project: finding the right builder for the reconstruction contract.

Being a government department, the PSA had to go through the process of competitive tendering, which implies the acceptance of the lowest quote. It is therefore of paramount importance that all builders invited to tender have the appropriate qualities to carry out the work. We were looking for a firm which had a high level of craft and building skills, financial stability, expert management, and above all, a sensitive and dedicated approach to work with historic buildings. It was important that this final criterion was met by management, staff and all associated operatives.

Experience shows that competitive tendering produces the cheapest, but not always the best builder. However, provided every contractor who was invited to submit a price fulfilled our requirements, we could confidently accept the lowest bid.

The working party made the following schedule:

1. An advertisement would be placed in the *EEC Journal* in order to include European companies in the selection process. The nature of the project would be described and applications invited from firms wishing to be given consideration.

The advertisement was published on 5 February 1987 and produced thirty-one responses from contractors. All were British.

2. By a comprehensive evaluation of the standing and reputation of the applicants, we would draw up a short list of eight to ten names. Each of these would be sent the Essential Brief, invited to visit the site and given unrestricted access to all drawings and specifications prepared at that stage. Answers to questions would be circulated to all contractors concerned.

The Essential Brief described the requirements, the restrictions and the context within which the project was to be carried out. This stage was reached by the end of July.

3. Each firm would then be asked to submit a methodology statement, setting out their detailed proposals for carrying out the work. From this, a selection of firms would be made for the penultimate stage, the interview.

Six firms reached this point and in the second week of November they arrived one by one, to spend half a day talking about their proposals for the project. The group included all the firm's key staff, from managing director to site agent. In the end, three firms – Higgs and Hill, Rattee and Kett, and James Longley – were put on the final tender list.

It had been a long process, but we were able to face 1988 secure in the knowledge that, whichever of the three was eventually given the job, we would have an excellent contractor for the restoration.

However, 1987 did not end without incident. The autumn brought an unexpected event which left a trail of devastation across the south of England: the great October Storm. The parks and gardens of the Palace suffered badly, with more than 500 mature trees blown down. The more pragmatic members of the team commented on the now ample supply of limewood.

The morning after the storm, 16 October, I walked most of the way to the Palace, and as I picked my way through the carpet of branches and roof tiles, my thoughts went to the flimsy-looking aluminium structure which we had erected over the fire-damaged shell. I looked around to see gaping holes in the roofs of solid thirties' suburban houses. Cars had been crushed by falling trees and the devastation was awesome.

As I crossed Hampton Court Bridge, my relief at seeing the unsightly metal construction still in place over the King's Apartments was immense. Much as we had wanted to be finished with it, its presence that morning was more welcome than at any time during the project.

I climbed onto the sloping aluminium surface and braced myself in the blustery wind. On all sides there were scenes of widespread damage and confusion. The gutters and down-pipes had gone and the clear panels had been sucked out. However, everything else was there, a bit curled up at the edges, but most definitely there.

We all breathed a huge sigh of relief, cleared up, checked the scaffolding and returned to our 900 drawings.

The birdcage scaffold (Crown Copyright)

(opposite) The high-level platform (Crown Copyright)

6 · Craftsmen and Contractors

No disaster, however destructive, is entirely without its creative side. This had been demonstrated, in the early days after the fire, by the ladies from Brighton, whose carving had so moved us, and was confirmed again in the aftermath of the 1987 storm.

Having decided to purchase the structural timbers in advance of the main contract, so that the builder would have a supply of well-seasoned wood by the time work was started, tenders were invited from a variety of saw mills around the country. Eden's of Norfolk were the successful tenderer, and when we went to inspect the timber at their mill, the supervisor told us that although most of the wood was local, some had come from the great oaks blown down in Sevenoaks, Kent.

Unfortunately it was not possible to identify the individual beams, otherwise I am sure they would have been marked with brass plaques. However, it is satisfying to know that somewhere in the roof of Hampton Court Palace, the trees from Sevenoaks are helping to support the new structure. As Sara Wurtzburg remarked in the journal *Construction Repair*: 'One destroyed piece of English heritage becomes the saviour of another.'

Her words could also apply to some other timbers which, with the help of Treve Rosoman from English Heritage, had been rescued from a seventeenth-century Huguenot chapel in London's Fournier Street. The chapel was being demolished and after complex negotiation and some difficult transport problems, Treve arranged for a number of huge beams to be delivered to Hampton Court. Two and a half years later, most of them had been cut, trimmed and reused in the framework at the top of the hidden stairs.

The hidden stairs, although indeed hidden, were not a new discovery. They are situated in the middle of the King's Apartments, but are enclosed within the central wall. There are doors at the top and bottom, but no access to the main floor. This was to allow courtiers to reach their rooms on the third floor without disturbing the King.

The staircase had been out of use for many years and few members of the public, or even the staff, knew of its existence. As a result of the fire, it has now been opened up, repaired and redecorated, although because of its awkward location, it is unlikely to form part of future guided tours.

However, in the spring of 1988 guided tours were still very much in the future.

The hectic schedule of drawing and specification-writing had now reached its climax and we were ready to invite the three builders to submit their formal tenders.

By this time Dove Brothers had successfully completed the repair of the stone balustrades, cornices and window surrounds. The work had been continuing steadily for sixteen months, and the skill of Dove's craftsmen had made the task of Lorna Turney, who supervised the repair, a rewarding one.

Like the beads in the crystal chandelier, each stone had been tested for internal flaws. Any cracks were reinforced with resin and glass-fibre, although in some cases the damage was too great and new stonework had to be incorporated.

The stonemasons had worked high on the parapets above Fountain Court through two long winters. On dark afternoons, visitors had often stopped and stared at the ghostly shadows thrown onto the sheeting enclosing the third-floor balustrades.

On 5 July 1988 the envelopes arrived containing the final tenders. Rattee and Kett were the highest, followed by Higgs and Hill, with James Longley the lowest. Subject to arithmetical checks, the contract for the restoration of Hampton Court Palace would be awarded to James Longley, a family-owned and run company which was, in 1988, celebrating its 125th anniversary.

The three tenders were very close and this indicated keen and realistic pricing. There was still VAT to be added, as well as additional costs for such things as carving, conservation, and ceiling restoration, which would be let as separate contracts by the PSA. When all these figures were added up, the total budget for the building repair came to nearly £9,700,000. The cleaning and conservation of curtains, tapestries, and furniture was the responsibility of the Curator, and as such was budgeted separately.

The contract with James Longley and Co. Ltd was signed on 30 August 1988. Once this was done, a number of other decisions could be made. The first was the layout, access to, and arrangement of the working area. A complicated restoration project requires a small community of offices, stores, workshops and canteens, none of which could be accommodated within the building. We wanted to encroach as little as possible into the gardens and it seemed sensible to situate all the necessary buildings to the south of the Palace.

We later discovered that Longley's carpentry workshop had been established on the same site as Wren's. It was tempting to suggest that Longley's men should be issued with seventeenth-century smocks. (Incidentally, this happened in 1991, when some of them took part in the Masquerade organized by the Palace to celebrate the 500th birthday of Henry VIII.)

Having arranged the working area in the most compact space possible, we tackled the sensitive problem of widening the Privy Gates.

The original intention had been to allow contractors' traffic access along the Bargewalk and through the Privy Garden. However, the Minister of State at the Department of the Environment, Lord Caithness, had disapproved of this plan, feeling that an unacceptable disturbance would be caused to the public, both on the riverside and in the garden.

A better option, he felt, was along the Broadwalk down the east side of the Palace, even though this meant widening the Privy Gates which had been built by Wren as part of his grand design for the gardens. We discussed the matter at great length with English Heritage, and informed the Richmond Planning Authority of our proposals. The approval of the Royal Household was obtained for the temporary removal of one of the ornate stone gate-posts for the duration of the contract.

Each stone was carefully taken down, photographed, numbered and crated, and the other gate-post encased in timber to prevent accidental vehicle damage. A couple of weeks later we were roundly taken to task by the local planning authority for 'wanton destruction' of an historic building. It was difficult to make a satisfactory response, but with the structure now back in place and no trace of damage, those earlier anxieties have proved unwarranted.

Longley began work on phase one of their three-year contract on 3 October 1988. The contract had been divided into two parts because there were still important decisions to be taken, which required the skilled input of the contractor.

In normal circumstances, a contract is designed to run for a fixed period, with various penalties built-in if the contractor fails to complete on time. The client, for his part, is required to make all details of the project available at the outset. In this case, however, there were many uncertainties when the contract was let, and to achieve this objective would have been almost impossible. By creating a two-phase contract, we were able to work with the contractor to resolve these uncertainties in the six months of phase one.

During this period we also completed the de-charring process, decided on the reuse of the timber, and English Heritage were able to complete their archeological investigations without impeding the main building work.

Longley's on-site team was led by Senior Site Manager Brian Mayne. A deceptively quiet and self-effacing man, Brian was to run the job with an iron discipline from start to finish. He came to Hampton Court direct from a prestigious project for Longley's at Eton College, where his work was held in high esteem. Eton's loss was very much Hampton Court's gain.

The overall success of a project is largely determined by the quality of leadership given by both the Site Manager and the Contracts Manager. In Longley's Michael Harrison we were fortunate to have the services of an excellent Contracts Manager. He was neither quiet nor particularly self-effacing, and his aggressive Bristolian wit contrasted strikingly with Brian's measured firmness. The partnership of Harrison and Mayne produced a colourful combination of imagination, humour, efficiency and the ability to inspire the highest standards

The Priory Gates

from their workmen. Although there was a long way to go, the scene looked set for a successful contract.

There were still, of course, many meetings to be battled through; strong letters to be written, disagreed with, and finally sorted out over stormy telephone calls; occasional temperamental outbursts to be calmed, and 2,385 architects' instructions to be issued.

In November, Longley's workmen became aware of the high-profile nature of the project, when their carpenter-foreman Rod Blackmore took part with Jim Brooks from the PSA, in a demonstration of the new drop-out hatches for BBC TV's 'Tomorrow's World' programme. The 'Tomorrow's World' team was interested in the application of modern scientific developments in the repair of historic buildings.

71

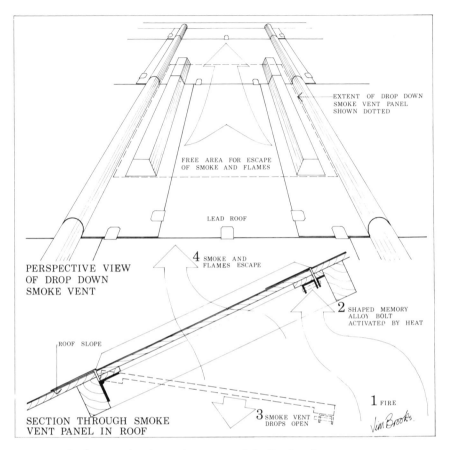

EXTENT OF DROP DOWN
SMOKE VENT PANEL
SHOWN DOTTED

FREE AREA FOR ESCAPE
OF SMOKE AND FLAMES

LEAD ROOF

PERSPECTIVE VIEW
OF DROP DOWN
SMOKE VENT

4 SMOKE AND
FLAMES ESCAPE

2 SHAPED MEMORY
ALLOY BOLT
ACTIVATED BY HEAT

ROOF SLOPE

1 FIRE

SECTION THROUGH SMOKE
VENT PANEL IN ROOF

3 SMOKE VENT
DROPS OPEN

Jim Brooks.

Diagram of a drop-out hatch (smoke vent panel) by Jim Brooks

The hatches were an innovation introduced as part of the improved fire protection of the building. It is interesting to note that the fire-brigade report on
the 1986 blaze had stated: 'Roof ventilation in itself was a major problem. It
took six men working with crowbars almost 20 minutes to roll back sufficient
of the lead sheet to facilitate space for cutting away the . . . close boarded roof
. . . The venting of the roof greatly eased conditions within the building.'

If we could build a mechanism into the structure which automatically provided such venting, the potential for damage caused by any future fire would
be greatly reduced. As a starting point for our design we looked at a system
of self-releasing hatches which had been developed after the fire at York Minster
in 1984.

The hatches designed for Hampton Court are also controlled by spring-operated bolts. The spring is made of a nickel titanium alloy, which has a 'memory', and at a temperature of 85°C straightens, drawing back the bolts on the hatch, which then drops open.

A mock-up of a hatch was built and over one hundred test runs were made to prove the mechanism. The prototype was then taken to the BBC studios. Rod Blackmore became a star for a day as he stood under the hatch with a hair dryer, heating up the spring. After thirty seconds, as the temperature reached 85°C, the hatch opened.

'Tomorrow's World' followed up this programme with another in March 1989, which featured the de-charring process and the use of sensors for moisture control. An area where dry rot had been discovered was filmed to show the potentially destructive effects which water can have. Presenter Peter McCann explained to viewers how the sensors were connected to a computer system which would allow future maintenance managers to monitor the moisture levels and spot immediately if a blocked gutter or burst pipe were leaking into the building.

Just as discoveries such as the handprints had provided a welcome diversion for the salvage team in the early days, the presence of television crews broke the normal building-site routine for Longley's workforce.

Throughout 1988, the search had continued for carvers and conservators who could be entrusted with the repair of the Grinling Gibbons carvings. By December a shortlist had been drawn up. The selection process involved looking at photographs and examples of completed work, visiting studios and workshops, and finally, conducting lengthy interviews with the craftsmen and women themselves.

We have often been asked whether we had difficulty finding craftsmen capable of carrying out the complex task of restoration. The answer is no. Traditional skills are far from dead and the time spent making an appointment was not because the right skills were hard to find, but rather that we were spoilt for choice.

The completion and re-dedication of the South Transept of York Minster was celebrated on 4 November 1988 and was proof of the skill and craftsmanship available within the building industry. The working party at Hampton Court sent its congratulations to Dr Charles Brown and his team. Their four-and-a-half years of restoration were an inspiration and, although we still had a long way to go, the prospect of a fully restored Hampton Court was becoming sharper in our minds.

(overleaf) Queen Post trusses in position (Crown Copyright)

7 · Restoration Begins

When Longley's started work on rebuilding the burnt-out wing in the autumn of 1988, the pigeons rapidly noticed the change. As the massive internal 'birdcage' scaffold rose through the building, the airspace in which they had been flying about for the past two and a half years was drastically reduced. Most gave up and flew away, but a few sat it out on nests among the chimneys. The builders allowed them to remain until their parental duties were complete; then eviction was swift.

Most rebuilding projects start at the bottom and work up, but at Hampton Court the situation was the reverse. Longley's started with the roof and moved down. To work at this high level, a large platform was needed and the internal 'birdcage' scaffolding served to support the deck with an impenetrable forest of poles.

Assembling a Queen Post truss

While the scaffolding was being erected the construction of the roof trusses began. There were two types of truss: the simple triangular type spanning about twenty-five feet, known as a King Post; and the flat-topped Queen Post which spans thirty-eight feet and stands eight feet high. The shape of each type of truss and its joints was drawn full-size and this became the pattern or 'rod' from which the timbers were cut. The trusses were assembled at ground level, much as Wren's workmen would have constructed them, with the joints held together by the salvaged wrought-iron brackets, which had been straightened in Richard Quinnell's forge in Leatherhead, Surrey. The bottom ties were made of Baltic Pine, while the upper timbers were of oak. It is said that Wren was forced to use pine for the bottom ties, because the demands of the shipbuilding industry at the time had created a shortage of oak beams long enough for his needs. We, in our turn, were unable to obtain Baltic Pine in the required lengths and the pine had to be supplied from Canada.

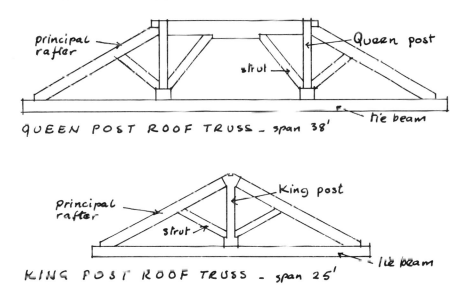

Each truss was checked, numbered and then dismantled to await the arrival of the crane which would lift the timbers to roof level. Longley's did not keep a crane permanently on site, which would have been both expensive and intrusive, but hired one when the need arose.

One of the first occasions when the crane was required was in March 1989, when the enormous third-floor beam which had crashed into the Cartoon Gallery was replaced. This had to be done before the roof was complete. The beam weighed over a ton, and the problem was to set it onto two existing bearings without knocking out any of the brickwork. The solution was to swing one end out of a window, then the other end back through an enlarged hole in

(opposite) King Post trusses in position (Crown Copyright); (above left) A charred roof truss with wrought-iron bracket (Crown Copyright); (above right) De-charred truss (Longley); (below) Laying the lead sheeting (Longley)

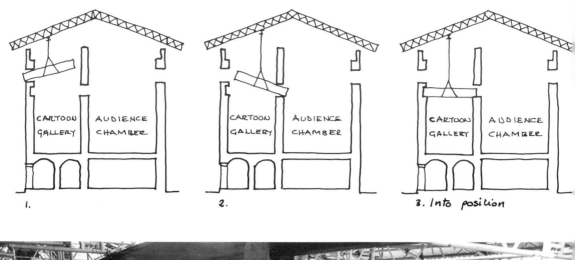

1. 2. 3. Into position

Installing the third-floor beam (Times Newspapers)

the central wall and lower the beam into its final position. The whole complex manoeuvre took four hours, and as the beam came to rest on its bearings, Brian Mayne gave an audible sigh of relief.

With the floor beam in place, work could continue on the roof. As truss after truss was put into place, the sweet smell of sawn oak began to replace the pungent odour of charred wood which had dominated the building since the fire. A deodorizing agent had neutralized some of the smell, and the de-charring process had helped. But for several years after the blaze, it was not unusual to catch an occasional sharp and acrid reminder of the fire.

While the roof construction was proceeding, excavations below ground uncovered the old culverts. A closed-circuit television survey was carried out, which involved dragging a camera through the hidden drains. The resulting video tape revealed arched brick culverts in reasonably good condition, but with a number of areas in need of repair.

The excavations provided an excellent opportunity for English Heritage to examine both the culverts and the seventeenth-century foundations which were discovered beside them. The archeological investigation produced other import-ant information, particularly from beneath the Large Oak Room. The floor had been removed for the installation of a new heating system and this had revealed evidence of the foundations of Henry VIII's and probably Cardinal Wolsey's palaces. This confirmed previous speculation about certain features of their layout.

A variety of rubble had been packed into these old foundations, among which were pieces of sixteenth-century terra cotta. It was surprising to find that the decoration on the fragments was more elaborate for the period than any pre-viously discovered at the Palace.

These and many of the other items found during the restoration were put on display in the Fire Damage Exhibition, which opened at the Palace at the end of 1988. The exhibition included a full-size model of the floor construction, complete with seashells, as well as a detailed scale model of the roof trusses, both made by Longley's apprentices.

By the end of 1989 the roof structure was nearing completion. Before long the entire King Post section was covered with boarding, and the laying of lead sheeting could begin. Work on the Queen Post section then followed. The lifting, forming and laying of the thick sheets is heavy work, with the lead weighing between seven and nine pounds per square foot. More than ninety-three tons of milled lead cover the new roofs, and the massive construction of the trusses below is needed to support this great weight.

(overleaf) Old foundations revealed under the floor in the Large Oak Room (Crown Copyright)

In addition to being heavy work, the laying of lead can be extremely hazardous. Great care was taken to ensure that lead burning presented the minimum fire risk, and a full-time fire-patrol officer was present throughout the entire operation. Work was halted two hours before the end of the normal working day, so the whole area could cool down before the site was vacated.

A nice finishing touch to this part of the project was the new rainwater head made by students at the Guildford College of Technology. They prepared a bed of sand onto which they poured molten lead. When it had set, the flat sheet was wrapped around a wooden mould and fashioned into the required shape. It was then completed with the date '1989' in bold relief on the front face.

While the work on the roof was proceeding, some of the most complicated, but least glamorous work, was beginning. This was the 'M and E', the mechanical and electrical, which is both difficult to design and expensive to install.

Introducing mechanical systems into an elegant historical building is particularly intrusive. For example, how do you run water pipes above a fine ceiling? What is the best way to drill cable holes in seventeenth-century brickwork or oak panelling? These conflicts require skilled co-operation between designers and contractors. Nonetheless, it is a shame that much of this work has to be hidden away under the surface, considering the care taken by the electrical and mechanical sub-contractors to clip their cables neatly to the walls and to find the most ingenious routes for their pipework.

It was decided to install a new underfloor heating system in the smaller ground-floor rooms, but only to replace the floor panels in the State Apartments with identical units. The heating system has been greatly improved by connecting it to a new management system. A central computer controls temperature and monitors the security and fire-detection systems. The network of cables, junction boxes and control panels, all vital to the successful working of the Palace, have been discreetly hidden.

As the project progressed, the Longley team became familiar figures around the Palace. Their consideration for the residents, guards and visitors earned them much respect. Equally well established was the PSA staff, joined in January 1989 by a new Project Architect, Dante Vanoli. Dan led the on-site team until completion and formed a lively partnership with the Longley Contract Manager, Michael Harrison. Their pugnacious collaboration was continued away from the site, when Dan led the PSA cricket team to victory in a match for the 'Hampton Court Ashes' – from a burnt beam, of course. In the best cricketing tradition, Michael and the Longley's team regained the 'Ashes' the following year.

8 · The Carvers

On 30 August 1989, the Hampton Court team was shocked to hear of a fire which had severely damaged the seventeenth-century National Trust house at Uppark in Sussex. This beautiful building had stood unchanged on the South Downs for more than 300 years.

The situation had certain similarities with that at Hampton Court. Both fires occurred in late-seventeenth-century buildings which contained irreplaceable works of art. Each was occupied at the time of the fire (in the case of Uppark, by the Fetherstonhaugh family, who had been there since 1747), and in both cases difficult decisions had to be taken about how to handle the restoration.

It was sad that another team of architects, restorers and conservators would have to go through the process of salvage and rescue from which the Hampton Court team had recently emerged. But it did mean that the English Heritage members of the Hampton Court working party were able to provide experienced advice to the rescue teams at Uppark, and early in 1990 the National Trust, with their consultants, came to the Palace for a valuable exchange of views. The discussions revived memories of 1986: the saturated debris, water streaming down the panelling, and the chaos during the early days of salvage.

It was a relief now to be working in clean, dry surroundings over which a sense of order prevailed. In the carving workshop, where the job of cleaning and repairing the Grinling Gibbons carvings was about to begin, the environment was one in which delicate restoration tasks could safely be undertaken.

Towards the end of 1988 we had set up a workshop for the carvers in one of the ground-floor rooms of the King's Apartments. The location was perfect. The windows onto the gardens provided good daylight and also meant the public could see in and watch the work in progress.

This workshop was adjacent to the main site, and therefore the carvers and builders could feel part of the same team, whether they were cutting huge beams or fashioning fragile limewood 'forget-me-nots'. It was a beautiful panelled room containing a fireplace, over which was a magnificent carved oak panel by Grinling Gibbons. Once again, restorers were working under the watchful eye of the 'Master'.

The carvings were now removed from their 'coffins', having been stored for more than three years. There had been thirty-one carvings on the walls of the King's Apartments on the day of the fire, and of those, thirty had survived.

(right) Encrusted Grinling
Gibbons carving before
cleaning (Cliff Birtchnell);
(below) Richard Hartley
copying a burnt original
(Crown Copyright);
(opposite) David Luard
cleaning the carvings (Derek
Cattani)

Twenty-nine of the original carvings were in limewood while the two from the Cartoon Gallery were in oak. The workshop of Grinling Gibbons was responsible for twenty-seven of the limewood pieces, with the remaining two carved by the little-known John Le Sage.

Le Sage's name appears on a bill to the Earl of Bristol dated 1690 and again in the Hampton Court accounts, when he was paid £70 11s 7½d for carving the overmantel drops in the First Presence Chamber. Why he was chosen for this work, in preference to Gibbons, remains something of a mystery.

Grinling Gibbons himself was born in Rotterdam in 1648 of English parents who settled in England when he was about nineteen. He was discovered by the diarist John Evelyn, working in a house on Deptford marshes. Evelyn recorded the occasion in his diary:

'I this day first acquainted his Majestie with that incomparable young man, Gibson [sic], whom I had lately found in an Obscure place, & that by meere accident, as I was walking neere a poore solitary thatched house in a field in our Parish neere Says-Court: I found him shut in, but looking into the Window, I perceiv'd him carving that large Cartoone or Crucifix of Tintorets, . . . I saw him about such a work, as for the curiosity of handling, drawing and studious exactnesse, I never in my life had seen before in all my travells.'

Evelyn brought the carver to the attention of Charles II, but to the diarist's disappointment, the King did not buy the young man's work and Gibbons went back to Deptford. Eventually, the King was convinced and commissioned Gibbons to carve a panel as a present for Cosimo III, the Grand Duke of Tuscany. The Cosimo Panel is one of the finest examples of English wood-carving and is now in the Pitti Palace in Florence.

Commissions, such as those at Cassiobury, Holme Lacey and Windsor, enabled Gibbons to build up a large workshop and when he was made Master Carver to the Crown in 1693, his wealth and reputation were assured.

Gibbons carved in a wide variety of materials, including oak and marble, but was an unrivalled master in the carving of lime (linden wood). His exuberant compositions of leaves, fruit, sheaves of wheat and flowers are works of great originality and beauty. Despite being a hard wood, lime is soft to carve; its fine grain allows the chisel to cut and undercut in all directions. The wood is light in colour, and when set against a dark background the carvings seem to float in space.

Of the surviving carvings, one was badly burnt, another less so but still severely damaged. The rest were scorched, broken, streaked with water and covered in ash. The scorching presented the carvers with some of their most difficult decisions. For example, when should charred pieces be cut out and renewed? Which original details could be repaired and left in place? If a new piece of carving was to be fixed to a charred section, was the charred wood firm enough to receive the new?

These decisions could not be made until the carvings had been properly cleaned and the first task was to find skilled and experienced conservators to carry out this process. The working party decided that, however good the reputations of the firms and individuals on our shortlist, final selection could only be made after examination of a piece of completed work.

A contract was drawn up in which each firm was paid to carry out a small amount of cleaning, up to a value of £1,000. Those whose work was considered satisfactory were then commissioned to finish the job on that particular piece. We were helped in our assessments by Frances Halahan from the City and Guilds Institute, who had been appointed to advise on conservation and cleaning.

As a result of this preliminary selection, the Exeter firm of Herbert Read was appointed to carry out the remainder of the cleaning. Ruth Davies, David Luard and later, Torquil McNeilage, arrived at the Palace to begin work.

After dusting and vacuuming, the delicate use of a fine blade loosened the heavier encrustation. This was followed by the application of solvents to remove stains and wax. Only small areas could be dealt with at a time, because each had to be cleaned and dried immediately to avoid dirt being absorbed into the timber.

Badly charred areas were consolidated by brushing on or injecting resin and when all the sections and overlays of a drop were cleaned they were passed to the carvers for repair.

The first cut, which marked the beginning of the recarving was made by the chisel of Richard Hartley. Carvers, of course, differ in stature and Richard's workbench was one of three specially made to suit the individual height of each carver. Richard, like David Esterly and Trevor Ellis, was self-taught and had a natural talent for working with limewood.

Each of the carvers was commissioned to carry out a specific task. Richard's was to re-carve the top section of an over-door drop from the Drawing Room. It was a relatively small piece, which took two months to complete. Richard proved to be a man of many talents and after finishing his work at Hampton Court, he left the world of fine woodwork to become the lead guitarist in a rock group.

The majority of the remaining work was shared by David Esterly and Trevor Ellis, both of whom spent many months at the Palace. David read English at Cambridge and first came into contact with the work of Grinling Gibbons when he went to see the carved altarpiece in St James's, Piccadilly. That visit changed David's life. As he put it: 'The scales fell from my eyes.'

At first, he planned a book about Gibbons, but realized he could not describe convincingly the foliage style of carving without an understanding of the techniques in practice. Buying some chisels, he retired to a cottage in Sussex and began to carve.

(above) David Esterly at work (Cliff Birtchnell); (right) The replacement for the lost seven-foot drop (Cliff Birtchnell); (opposite) Detail of the replacement (Cliff Birtchnell)

Now, eighteen years later, he had become one of the foremost exponents of limewood foliage carving and his flamboyant overmantels grace many a fireplace in the United States. He does not copy Gibbons, but introduces his own creative ideas, incorporating wild flowers and even vegetables into the designs. A charming feature of his work is the beetle holes and ragged, caterpillar chewed leaves which appear in his compositions.

His task at Hampton Court however, was to copy exactly the work of Gibbons and to recreate the lost seven-foot drop, using as a reference a tiny fragment of burnt limewood and a full-size enlargement of a photograph taken before the war by a prudent civil servant.

Working from photographs is difficult for carvers because the two-dimensional black-and-white prints give no real idea of depth. Gibbons exaggerated the size of his fruit and flowers so that when seen from floor level they would appear in their natural scale. Calculating these proportions from a photograph was no easy matter.

The final result is quite breathtaking. The new drop is a profusion of leaves, apricots, ears of wheat, forget-me-nots, crocuses, pea-pods, laurel leaves, apples, pears, tulips, twining stems, and curving petals. It must be one of the finest pieces of carving carried out in England in recent years and is a noble replacement of the carving destroyed in the fire.

The working party established the principle that there should be no speculative carving. If a flower or some other detail did not appear in the photograph, it was not to be invented for the purpose of the repair. There were a number of instances of lost detail, possibly where pieces had been knocked off by cleaners or decorators, but unless there was indisputable evidence of what had existed before, no replacement was made.

The recarving process generated many new ideas about Grinling Gibbons and his methods. David had long held the view that Gibbons left his work exactly as it came from the chisel, with the surfaces formed by the hundreds of facets left by the carver's blade. However, under close inspection, it was found that the carvings had been finished and rounded off by using some kind of abrasive technique, such as sandpaper. But sandpaper had not been invented in the seventeenth century.

David had several ideas and experimented with a piece of leather sprinkled with pumice, and with the dried skin of a shark, which is certainly rough enough to act as an abrasive. Under the microscope, however, the tiny surface scratches did not match those on Gibbons's carvings.

Eventually, after many trials, David was referred by a musical intrument restorer to a plant called Dutch Rush (*Equisetum hyemale*). This absorbs silica from the soil and deposits it in nodules on the stem of the plant. It is uncommon in England and was imported in large quantities from Holland in the sixteenth and seventeenth centuries, when it was used for scouring. A trial with dried

Dutch Rush, rubbed on the limewood, produced surface marks exactly matching the originals.

David worked at Hampton Court for twelve months, the first two of which were spent studying photographs and planning the work. The remaining ten months were devoted to carving.

The third member of the carving team was Trevor Ellis. Formerly a member of the Royal Air Force and before that, the Royal Navy, he became a carver of ships' figureheads, fairground decorations, as well as Corinthian capitals and classical detail.

Trevor's brief was different from David's, but equally demanding. He was asked to repair and recarve the badly burnt over-door drop from the King's Audience Chamber. Like David, he worked from a full-size photograph and charred fragments, fashioning scores of details which then had to be fixed back onto the original carving. He also carved substantial new sections where the timber had either been completely destroyed or was beyond consolidation.

After completing the main drop, Trevor went on to repair and restore the other twelve carvings from the Audience Chamber and Drawing Room. It was an enormous undertaking and Trevor continued working for the two full years up to the handover.

The establishment of a 'School of Fine Carving' at Hampton Court had worked to perfection. The exchange of ideas and experience between carvers and conservators, and the informed comments from the many experts who visited the workshop, combined to create a centre of excellence, itself an acknowledgement of Gibbons's genius.

Three other carvers made a significant contribution to the success of the restoration. Roger Board worked on the drops in the First and Second Presence Chambers, Neil Trinder tackled four other pieces from the same rooms and Laurence Beckford from Herbert Read restored the extremely fragile Le Sage carvings. Laurence also worked on the two oak overmantels from the Cartoon Gallery and four other limewood drops.

It was a unique achievement and all six carvers realized that this was an episode in their professional lives which would probably never be repeated.

There was one final stage: colouring and waxing, which was carried out by Ellie Ellis and Simone Boux. The new, white limewood and the blackened consolidated timber were given four coats of acrylic paint, carefully applied to match the colour and grain of the unburnt lime.

Acrylics, which are water soluble, were used so that the principle of reversibility was maintained. At any time in the future, if conservation ideas change, the paint can be washed off and the 1990 repairs exposed.

The last job before rehanging was to apply a coat of micro-crystalline wax as a protective coating. This was a long, painstaking process which demanded great concentration and patience.

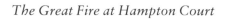

Trevor Ellis with a repaired carving (Cliff Birtchnell)

(above) David Luard giving the finishing touches (Longley)

(left) A restored carving showing integration of new and old limewood, before colouring and waxing (Trevor Ellis)

Trevor and Ellie Ellis (Paul Bernhardt)

When the carvings were rehung, the positional errors which we had discovered earlier were corrected. Today the carvings can, once again, be seen as Gibbons intended.

Trevor Ellis's work at Hampton Court received recognition when, in 1991, he was made an Honorary Freeman of the Worshipful Company of Joiners and Ceilers. It was a pleasing continuity with the past; an earlier Freeman of the Company had been Richard Rydge, the carver who in 1533 had carved the bosses of the Great Hall for Henry VIII.

(above) The restored
cornice in the Cartoon
Gallery (Longley);
(left) Refixing the
capitals in the
Cartoon Gallery
(Longley)

97

9 · *Topping Out*

1990 began with the second big storm to hit the southeast in three years and, as in 1987, trees were uprooted, fences flattened and roofs damaged. Fortunately the roof over the Palace survived, but Uppark was not so lucky. In its exposed position the fire-damaged house was particularly vulnerable to high winds and, tragically, its temporary roof was blown off, killing two workmen.

It was a sad reminder of the collapse at Hampton Court in 1689, when two of Christopher Wren's workmen were killed. The building industry has always been a hazardous one and things have changed little over the centuries. Thankfully, the restoration of Hampton Court after the 1986 fire was completed with a 100 per cent safety record.

April brought happier news, when the building was 'topped out'. Topping out is the traditional ceremony in the construction industry which marks the completion of the roof or highest point of a building. The owner is invited to lay the last tile, fix the final chimney pot, or in the case of Hampton Court, tap home the last clip securing the lead sheeting. This has two very tangible benefits. The structure is made watertight and the owner, to express his satisfaction with progress, provides tankards of ale for the workers.

The Duke of Gloucester, The Queen's cousin, performed this duty on behalf of the 'owner' and the cheers of the workmen were accompanied by the clicking of cameras. In his speech, he thanked Longley's workforce and referred to the enthusiasm which the British have for their heritage. He went on to say: 'It is a great tragedy when a building like this one is damaged by fire. I know this isn't the first . . . and I fear it won't be the last. But the important thing . . . is that it should be restored and replaced to be as similar as possible to what was there before . . . so that future generations . . . will feel that this is the real Hampton Court, not a modern version, not an improved version, but as authentic a building as the one conceived by Sir Christopher Wren.'

(opposite) Topping Out – HRH The Duke of Gloucester (centre) taps the last lead clip into place, 23 April 1990 (Longley)

(above) The completed
First Presence Chamber
at handover (Longley);
(right) The completed
Cartoon Gallery at
handover (Longley)

Repairs in the King's Drawing Room (Crown Copyright)

The topping out ceremony was preceded by the removal of the temporary roof. For the first time in four and a half years sunlight flooded onto the fine leadwork, and visitors during the summer of 1990 were able once again to enjoy the elegant balustrades and parapets over Fountain Court. However, although the exterior of the Palace looked nearly normal, inside the building there was still much to do.

With the building now weather-tight, work on the interior could proceed rapidly. The birdcage scaffold was still in place, but shrinking all the time. It greatly obstructed work in the State Apartments and therefore its final removal was a high priority. One of the last major jobs requiring the scaffold was the reinstatement of the ceilings and cornices.

Most of the ceilings were made of lath and plaster. Laths are thin strips of split chestnut about one inch wide. These are nailed to the underside of the ceiling joists, leaving a gap of about a quarter of an inch between each lath. This gap forms a 'key' into which the plaster is pressed, thus holding it in position.

The first coat of plaster is mixed with animal hair, traditionally horse or goat, and this forms a loose matting in the plaster, preventing it from crumbling. The design team discussed what type of hair should be used and it was decided to go for a mixture of sisal (a plant fibre) and a smaller amount of goat hair. This seemed to be a reasonable twentieth-century compromise.

Although many areas were repaired in this way it was not possible to use traditional lath and plaster for every ceiling, simply because of the size of the area to be covered and the difficulty of obtaining adequate quantities and lengths of split laths. Splitting is a manual process carried out by only a few small firms around the country. Each lath is split individually by driving a blade down the full length of the wood.

Longley's became irritated at the delay and after many enquiries, they were advised by one supplier not to be so impatient: 'The maximum length of the laths . . . is governed by the height of the craftsmen splitting the timber.' Michael Harrison, not the tallest of men, responded promptly and to the point: 'the height formula may also be applicable to a Contract Manager's temper control level.'

In the end, expanded metal lathing had to be used for the ceiling of the Cartoon Gallery. This vast area of plaster measuring 117 feet by 24 feet could not possibly have been completed on time using chestnut laths. It was a disappointment, but one of the few occasions when historical integrity had to give way to practical necessity.

The last job for the birdcage scaffolding involved the reinstatement of the oak cornices in the Cartoon Gallery. Their repair had been like trying to solve a giant jigsaw puzzle.

The bewildering collection of salvaged fragments was examined and the

Lath and plaster ceiling (Cliff Birtchnell)

entire 117 foot length of the cornice drawn full-size by Longley's 'setter-out'.
By this means, exact measurements could be made of all the individual pieces,
both damaged and undamaged. Any sections missing altogether could be identified at a glance and these would be replaced. Joiners then cut, carved and fitted
the new pieces into the existing body of the cornice.

In the process of carrying out this exercise, it was discovered that Wren's
mathematical planning of the room had not been translated exactly into practice. The twelve window bays varied by as much as one inch and the seventeenth-
century carpenters had cleverly stretched the carved detail between each pilaster
to make up the difference.

With the cornices in position, the birdcage scaffold was finally dismantled
and the interiors of the State Apartments began to resume their former appearance. The installation of electrical wiring, refixing of oak panelling, and repairs
to the floors could now proceed at full speed.

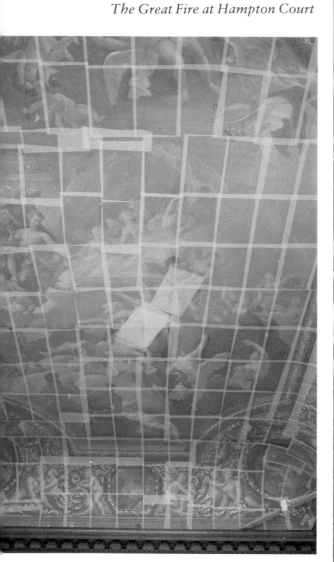

(above) Antonio Verrio's painted ceiling in King William's Bedroom, protected by pieces of 'Mulberry' (tissue) paper (Crown Copyright); (right) Completing the restoration of the painted ceiling (Cliff Birtchnell)

The work on the floors provided a further opportunity to put back some original construction features. Wren had used pine floorboards in a random variety of widths, some very wide by modern standards. Many had since been replaced with narrow tongued and grooved oak boarding which considerably changed the character of the room. Consistent with the overall restoration policy, it was decided to return to the original design.

We knew the width of each of the seventeenth-century boards because Wren's carpenters had cut notches in the tops of the floor joists to receive fillers, which were laid under the join of each floorboard. By measuring the distance between these notches, we were able to order new boards of the same random widths as those used by Wren.

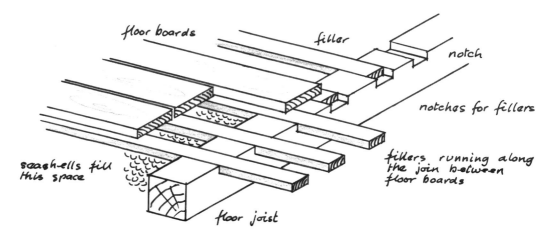

The floorboards are unfinished, exactly as they were 300 years ago. Lengthy trials were carried out in an attempt to find an applied finish which would protect them, yet still retain the texture and quality of the untreated timber. This proved impossible and we reluctantly had to agree with the Curator that the synthetic nature of all the samples we tried was quite unsatisfactory. It had been his original intention to leave the floors untreated for historical reasons, and he decided ultimately that regular cleaning and natural wear would produce the best long-term results.

Under the floorboards, the seashells were carefully replaced in the spaces between the joists. Longley must be the only builder to have employed a 'seashell washer' on their staff, and the washing took place in a special tank designed by Michael Harrison.

The seashells back in position between the fillers (Crown Copyright)

Repairing the throne canopy (Derek Cattani)

HM The Queen on the roof, 8 April 1991 (Cliff Birtchnell)

The pace of conservation and repair was increasing rapidly, both on and off the building site. Most of the water-damaged pictures had been cleaned and restored at the Hamilton Kerr Institute, while the weaving and dyeing of silk damask for the curtains and wall hangings was about to begin.

The conservators, meanwhile, were regilding the gold and silver carved bosses from which the chandeliers were to be suspended. The crystal chandelier, which had been restored by Delomosne, was now back at the Palace, packed in crates, awaiting reassembly and hanging.

The cleaners and carvers working on the Grinling Gibbons drops spent long hours at their benches, while at the same time patiently answering questions from members of the public through the windows of their workshop.

In the Textile Conservation Studios, the rescued hangings and canopies from the King's Chairs of State had been cleaned and were under repair. The washing of the tapestries was about to begin.

The textile studio was established at Hampton Court in 1912 by H.C. Marillier who was the partner and successor of William Morris. The fires of 1882 and 1886 had focused attention on the need for conservation facilities and the textile studio was set up as a result. It continued under Morris & Co. management until 1947, when it was sold to the Ministry of Works. Its latest acquisition is a fully mechanized washing tank and this has greatly improved working conditions. For many years, Jenny Band and her team had been seen either barefoot or in Wellington boots in one of the courtyards, hosing down tapestries, which had been laid flat on the stone paving.

In the Cartoon Gallery, the twenty-six carved-oak Corinthian capitals, for which Gibbons had been paid £152 in 1690, were now back on top of their pilasters. The broken and burnt acanthus leaves had been replaced and the capitals hoisted into position. These repairs had been carried out in the Putney workshop of Roger Board. At this stage, the cornices and capitals presented a patchwork of dark, original timber and light coloured repairs. Staining, blending and polishing were still to come.

Even at this stage, the daily routine on-site was regularly brightened by new discoveries. On the underside of a piece of oak boarding a message was found: 'John Trevethan, Joseph Puckeridge, John Gordon, journeymen to Mr Fuller White, carpenter in Weybridge, relaid this floor, June 1758.'

The accuracy of the date has been questioned, as the floorboard on which the inscription appears shows evidence of machine as well as hand crafting. If local records are ever traced of 'Mr Fuller White, carpenter in Weybridge', it may eventually be possible to authenticate the date and the names.

(opposite) Silver-gilded carved boss by Trevor Ellis for the Audience Chamber

(above) The reinstated 'sideboard' in the Large Oak Room (Cliff Birtchnell); (right) Detail of the replacement rail of the 'sideboard' (Cliff Birtchnell)

112

(left) Lettering found on the underside of a piece of oak boarding in the Large Oak Room (Crown Copyright); (below) Note and cocoa-tin container found beneath the floor of the Guard Chamber (Joan Jones)

A note was also found hidden in a cocoa tin under the floor of the Guard Chamber. It credited Reginald Jenkins, Alfred Sturgis and George Hunt with the laying of the floor in 1911. Another discovery was a subscription list left in the Cartoon Gallery, giving the names of twenty-nine workmen who contributed to a leaving present of tobacco, brandy and money for a colleague called George Woodward. Mr Woodward sailed for the Transvaal in January 1900, possibly to fight in the Boer War.

The list ends with the name of 'Foreman Mr Cook', after which one of the men has added the words, 'who we regret has turned out an ill-disposed man'. It seems that Mr Cook, unlike Alf Barron, our own Clerk of Works, was less than successful in winning the respect of his men.

10 · Handover

In April 1991, Her Majesty The Queen visited Hampton Court to inspect the progress of the project and to meet the workmen. What was particularly enjoyable about the visit was its informality. She spent an hour and a half at the Palace, during which time she climbed onto the roof. Standing among the chimney pots, wearing the obligatory safety helmet, she inspected the new lead work, before going inside the roof space to examine the great oak beams and the drop-out hatches. She commented on the structure, the brickwork, the wrought iron and the achievements of Sir Christopher Wren himself.

Downstairs, Her Majesty handled and admired the Grinling Gibbons carvings, and remarked on the sadness of her last visit on the day of the fire. In the Small Oak Room she compared her own hands with the prints in the plaster. The Queen was particularly interested in the staining and polishing of the oak panelling. At the time of her visit, the new panels were being refixed next to scorched, blackened and undamaged pieces. The stainers had to apply different treatments to each area to produce a perfect match, while at the same time achieving a faithful and accurate colour.

The panelling in each apartment had its own distinct tone; in the Cartoon Gallery, rich and dark; in the Oak Rooms, a mellow honey colour, and in the Audience Chamber, a medium brown. It was important to restore the individual character of each room. By rubbing or brushing on the stain, a harmonious balance was achieved between the new and old sections. Then the polishers took over, applying liberal quantities of beeswax, which was burnished. This left the panelling lustrous and sweet smelling.

In King William's Bedroom a scaffold was erected so Antonio Verrio's painted ceiling could be restored. After the fire, it was feared that the ceiling would collapse under the weight of water and emergency plans were made to erect a high platform, on which large balloons could be inflated to support the plaster. Fortunately, the ceiling steadily dried out, the danger of collapse receded and the balloons were unnecessary. However, the surface of the paint had begun to peel, and we decided to cover the whole area with pieces of 'Mulberry' (tissue) paper to hold the paint in position.

Now, five years later, it was the moment to soak off the paper, stick back the peeling paint, and finally restore the painting itself. The work was undertaken by Jan Keevil's picture restoration team from English Heritage, who took two and a half months to complete the job. Seeing the fully-restored work, which appropriately depicts themes of sleep, it is apparent how great the loss would have been had the plaster fallen.

The Large Oak Room was another of William's rooms whose restoration was now being completed. It had originally been the King's private dining room, and before the fire the PSA had intended to reinstate the 'sideboard', a small serving area demolished to make way for a stage when the apartment was turned into a meeting room at the beginning of this century. The reconstruction of the 'sideboard' was now included in the fire damage project, consistent with the policy of restoring as much as possible of the Palace's original fabric.

The 'sideboard' had a black-and-white marble floor, and had been separated from the dining room by a carved rail, with balusters and opening gates of which no record existed. It was decided, therefore, to model the replacement on the altar rail in the Chapel Royal at the Palace. The result is that, for the first time in many years, the public can see this room furnished as the King's private dining room, complete with its silver-filled sideboard.

Inside the Palace was not the only area where reconstruction was going on. In the grounds, the foundations of the steps which had once led to the raised walkway beside the Privy Gardens were found under the South Terrace. The steps were rebuilt according to their original design, returning the terrace to its former appearance. This discovery was exciting, particularly as this was a time when so many things were disappearing: the majestic roof trusses were now completely enclosed in the spaces between the lead sheeting and the plaster ceilings; the seashells, beams, joists, battens and fillers were out of sight beneath the floors.

By the middle of 1991 we began to put together all the drawings and handbooks which would be passed to the Palace Administrator, Crawford Macdonald, at the completion of the project. These included reduced copies of the drawings prepared for the contract, as well as operating manuals for the electrical and mechanical systems; instruction books for the central management computer; details about the drop-out hatches; names, addresses and telephone numbers of the 248 suppliers and sub-contractors; copies of their guarantees, test certificates and specifications. In other words, everything that a maintenance manager would need to run the building. And just so he or she would be fully informed, we also included notes of our failures, such as the fourteen treatments which had been tried on the new pine floorboards, and subsequently rejected.

The quantity surveyor provided some impressive statistical information. A total of 460,800 nails and 167,800 screws had been used in the restoration; the electricians had laid 27,819 metres of cable; the polishers applied 545 litres of methylated spirit and 22,725 litres of hot water, and rubbed their way through

3,000 sheets of sandpaper. The parapets contained twenty-seven tons of new Portland Stone and a further three tons of marble had gone into repairing the floors.

We summarized the improvements which had been introduced as part of the restoration. These included the reinstatement of original features, such as the pine floorboards, South Terrace steps and Large Oak Room 'sideboard', as well as fire-protection improvements, such as the drop-out hatches, the extension of the automatic detection system, the introduction of fire stopping behind wall panelling and in floors, and the increased 'compartmentation' (the division of the building into sections, each surrounded by fire-protected walls).

Unmentioned in our documents are the messages, signatures and mementoes undoubtedly hidden in the building by Longley's workmen, following in the tradition of their seventeenth-century (and later) predecessors. A more formal record for posterity was the 'time capsule'. It contained a copy of *The Times* from 1 April 1986, photographs of Longley's workforce, a fragment of burnt Grinling Gibbons carving together with a small piece of replacement, and many other items. The capsule itself was made from oak from one of the roof trusses, and only Brian Mayne and Jim Brooks know where it is hidden. It is hoped it will remain undiscovered for many, perhaps hundreds, of years.

Longley was due to complete its contract by midnight 2 October 1991. Michael Harrison scrutinized every architect's instruction for any hint of change which might cause delay. Meantime the arrangements for the day itself were well advanced. Baroness Blatch, Minister for the Heritage, would accept the finished work after a formal declaration from the PSA that the contract had been completed properly. Responsibility for the site would then pass from Longley to the Palace Administrator, who would arrange the return of the furniture, paintings, curtains and tapestries. Simon Thurley, Curator of the Historic Royal Palaces Agency, would in practice control the work.

The final cost of the contracts for the restoration of the building was about £8.5 million, about £1.2 million under budget. This does not include the professional fees and the cost of refurnishing, which were budgeted for separately.

Wednesday 2 October arrived and the restoration was complete. At 3.30 p.m., eight and a half hours ahead of the expiry of the contract, Baroness Blatch opened the door to the State Apartments, with a specially-made brass key. To Michael Harrison's immense relief it did not jam or snap in the lock and the door swung gently open.

Ernest Law, who was a grace-and-favour resident at Hampton Court from 1895 to 1930, loved its many moods and seasons, and in his history of the Palace wrote: 'It is at night that the Palace . . . is invested with its most romantic garb . . . it would be difficult to match the exquisite beauty of the picturesque old courts, gables, towers, and turrets, when their broken outline stands out against a sky bathed in the radiance of the rising moon; or the poetic aspect

of the Fountain Court, when the moonbeams shoot down upon the water of the circular fountain in its midst, glitter on the panes of the old window, or mingle with the lights that blink and flicker through the arches of the arcade beneath; while all night through the sound of the cool trickle of the fountain soothes the air.'

Some of those most closely involved in the project were fortunate to experience something of the atmosphere described by Ernest Law when, on the evening before the handover, Crawford Macdonald gave a supper party in the Banqueting House. After coffee, we walked across the moonlit gardens to Fountain Court. The great rooms were silent and bathed in a gentle light. The oak panelling gleamed and the Gibbons carvings seemed to float above our heads. The evening was my third unfading memory of the project. The first had been the day of the fire itself, the second the devastation seen from the top of the aluminium roof after the 1987 storm, and the third was this magical impression of the finished apartments at midnight on the day before the handover.

Following the handover, the furnishing of the rooms could proceed. Simon Thurley had found copies of the Raphael Cartoons rolled up in the basement of the Ashmolean Museum in Oxford. They had probably been made by Henry Cooke when he was repairing the originals for William III. They have been completely restored and now hang in the Cartoon Gallery. In the Audience Chamber, the crystal chandelier once again glitters beneath its silver-gilded boss.

The Apartments can be seen today very much as William saw them for the first time, complete and furnished, on 17 November 1699. The result represents the dedication of hundreds of people whose work embodied conservation skills of the highest order. In an age when it is often assumed that traditional crafts are fast dying out, it is encouraging that so much of this work was carried out by young people. Wren would surely have appreciated their achievements.

There is one other group of 'workers' whose contribution has so far gone unrecognized. In his final statistics, the quantity surveyor calculated that sixty-four kilograms of beeswax had been used to polish the restored oak panelling. He added: 'With one hive containing an average of 60,000 bees, producing an average of 2.3 kilograms of wax in a normal year, a total of 27.83 hives was required. That is 1,670,000 bees producing full time for one year.'

Sir Christopher Wren would surely have approved of that too.

(opposite) The author with Baroness Blatch in King William's Bedroom, 2 October 1991 (The Guardian); (overleaf) The restoration team and the workforce (Longley)

Appendices

Appendix I The Salvage Squad 31 March 1986

Joe Cowell *Superintendent of the Royal Collection*
Jesse Daniels *Verger of the Chapel Royal*
Fred Allen *Stonemason*
Craig Cowell *Student*
Simon Cowell *Student*
Graham Cowell *Student*
Richard Evans *Propagator*
Alan Hubbard *Foreman*
Bob Hunt *Storeman*
Ted Salisbury *Joiner*
Les Strudwick *Gardener*

Appendix II The Working Party

At the initial meeting on 3 April 1986

Michael Fishlock *Project Manager PSA*
Gerald Drayton *District Works Officer PSA*
Lorna Turney *Architect PSA*
David Utting *Architect PSA*
Martin Funnell *Principal Architect (Survey) PSA*
Alastair Bond *Executive Officer PSA*
Juliet West *Inspector English Heritage*
John Thorneycroft *Architect English Heritage*
Ian Gray *Superintendent Hampton Court Palace*
Glyn George *Deputy Superintendent Hampton Court Palace*

Who were joined at subsequent meetings by:

PSA
Ron Barlow
Alf Barron
Lincoln Baskett
Jim Brooks
Ray Brookshaw
Colin Brown
Danny Canniffe
Ron Cox
Jonathan Crow
Den Davies
Grant Elliott
Brian Fairweather
Giovanna Garrino
Graham Goode
Margaret Gray
D. J. Green
Nick Green
Nick Healey
Murray Jervis
Stuart Laing
Simon Leach
Charles Mangles
Ray Marshall
Fred Mellings
Peter Nickels
Cliff Nursey
Hedley Pavett
Steve Russell
Bob Sandford
Laurie Smith
Sheila Stirrit
Tony Talbot
Peter Taylor
Derek Tidy
Malcolm Tomlinson
Dan Vanoli*

Steve Wagstaffe*
Brian Wise
David Woods Taylor*

English Heritage
David Batchelor
Peter Curnow

Historic Royal Palaces Agency
Jenny Band (*formerly PSA*)
Val Davies (*formerly PSA*)
Daphne Ford (*formerly English Heritage*)
Simon Thurley (*formerly English Heritage*)

Central Office of Information
Adrian Antrum
Judy Davidson

Consultants
Lawrence Clarke
Michael Coates
Philip Cook
Len Davis
Alan Guy
Graham Holmes
Ted Kilby
Stuart Pack
Jeff Prossor
Brian Ridout
Paul Rosa
Brian Sheppard
Richard Spencer
Ron Stenning
David Stokoe
Alan Swettenham

*Project Architects

Appendix III Principal Consultants

Quantity Surveyor	Leonard Stace Partnership
Services Engineers	Jackson Stokoe Partnership
Timber Decay Specialists	Hutton and Rostron
	Ridout Associates
Building Surveyors	Stirling Surveys
Timber adviser	Timber Research and Development Association
Lead adviser	Lead Sheet Association
Photogrammetric Surveyors	Plowman Craven Associates
Conservators	Carvers and Gilders
	Herbert Read
	Plowden Smith Associates
	Neil Trinder
	Nicola Ashurst
	West of England Studios
	Adriel Consultancy

Appendix IV NADFAS Volunteers

Veronica Baker
Didie Bucknall
Ruth Carruthers
Ruth Cole
Maureen Critchel
Lindsey Graham

Paulette Hart
Jean Martin
Marny Park
Ann Stevenson
Beryl Tunnicliffe
Joyce Wilmot

Appendix V Donors

Miss H. R. Bach

M. & Mme Bernard

Leslie Butcher

Leon S. Cahn

E. & J. Carter

Mrs J. M. Chard

Mark O. Clampitt

Christine Edward

Greg Ford

Mrs Evelyn Frey

James A. Goldsmith Jnr

Norman Hansen

Harold Johnson

Mrs L. Krausz

Edgar E. Lawley Foundation

J. A. MacDonald

Ray McNaught

Harlyn and Virginia McNeil

G. & J. Mutton

Mrs W. R. Myers

R & I Tours

Robert and Elizabeth Ryan

R. Philip Smart

Snyder Research Laboratories Inc.

Anon, Staffordshire

Stratford (Ontario) Shakespeare Festival
    Foundation

Owen and Margaret Tabor

Mrs Carol Thornlow

Toledo Museum of Art, Ohio

Estelle and John Troup & family

Mary Wesbrook

West Surrey National Trust Centre

Patricia Whitesides

Mr & Mrs Thomas Whitesides

Miss Hilda Wilson

Mrs L. A. Young

Appendix VI Species of Fungus and Shells

Fungus and Moulds

Basidiomycetes (decay fungi)
    Coprinus sp.
    Serpula lacrymans (dry rot)

Hyphomycetes (moulds)
    Aspergillus sp.
    Chrysosporium sp.
    Penicillium sp.
    Trichoderma sp.
    Stachybotrys atra

Ascomycetes (plaster moulds)
    Peziza sp.
    Pyronema sp.

Myxomycetes (slime moulds)
    Stemonitis splendens

Shells

Cerastoderma edule (cockle) : formed majority of pugging
Mytilus edulis (mussel)
Macoma balthica (no common name)
Abra alba (no common name)
Nassarius reticulatus (netted dog whelk)
Littorina littorea (winkle)
These are typical of shells which would be found in a muddy estuary.

Index

Figures in italics refer to captions

archeology 40, 57, 61, 70, 81
Audience Chamber *16*, 18, 39, 93, *111*, 119

BBC 39, 63, 71, 73
Bailey, Mrs 14, *15*, 42
Baker, Rt Hon Kenneth 18
Band, Jenny 18, 58, 111
Banqueting House 59, 119
Bargewalk 69
Barron, Alf 114
Batchelor, David 40
Beckford, Laurence 93
Bettina 49, 51
Blackmore, Rod 71, 73
Blatch, Baroness 117, *119*
Board, Roger 93, 111
Boux, Simone 93
Brett, A. J. 42
Broadwalk 70
Brooks, Jim 39, 71, 72, 117

Caithness, Lord 70
Cartoon Gallery 12, 13, *16*, 18, 30, 40, 52, 88, 93, 97, *100*, 102, 111, *114*, 115, 119
carvers
  selection of 73
  workshop 85 (*see also* under individual names)
carvings
  cleaning 86, 89; colouring 93; Cosimo Panel 88; Dutch Rush 92; finishing 93; recarving policy 92; rehanging 96; removal for storage 52; repairs 85, 88, 89, 92, 93; salvage 36; wrong positions 53, *53*, 96
ceilings
  Cartoon Gallery 102; lath and plaster 102, *103*; King's Bedroom *104*, 115
Central Office of Information (COI) 39, *40*
Chambers, William 34
chandelier 18, 39, 40, *41*, 42,

111, 119
Chapel Court 28
Chapel Royal 18, 116
Charles, HRH The Prince of Wales 9, *16*, 18
Charles I, King 13
Charles II, King 88
Cloister Green Apartments 61
Cloister Green Court 28
collapse, 1689 building 28, 57, 58, 61, 99
contract 69, 70
Cosimo, Grand Duke of Tuscany 88
Cosimo Panel 88
Cowell, Joe 18, 39, 58

damp control 38, 39, 73
Daniels, Jesse 58
Davies, Ruth 89
de-charring 36, 37, 60, 70, 73, 79, 81
Delomosne and Son 40, 111
donations 54, 63
Dove Brothers 56, 57, 69
Downes, Professor Kerry 51
Drawing Room 53, 89, 93, *101*
Drayton, Gerald 13, 19, 35
drop-out hatches 71, 72, *72*, 73, 115, 117
Dutch Rush 92–3

electrical work 60, 84, 103
Elizabeth II, HM Queen 18, 30, 99, *109*, 115
Ellis, Ellie 93, 96
Ellis, Trevor 54, 89, 93, 94, 96, *96*
English Heritage 18, 35, 36, 38, 40, 57, 58, 61, 68, 70, 81, 85, 115
Esterly, David 43, 52, 53, 54, 89, *90*, 92, 93
Evelyn, John 88

fibre optics 39
finds 45, 46, 47, 48, 49, *50*, 52,

81, 111, 114
Fingerprint Society 49, 51
Fire
  A. J. Brett 42, *43*; cause of 1986 14, 30, 31; description of 1986 11, 12, 13, 14, *15*, 18, 19, 30–31; 1882 29; 1886 28, 29, *29*; first anniversary 63; new protection 72, 117; Uppark 85; York Minster 72
Fire brigade 11, 12, 18, 30, 31, 39, 72
Fire Damage Exhibition 54, 81
First Presence Chamber 88, 93, *100*
Ford, Daphne 38
Fountain Court 11, *12*, 28, *34*, 69, 102, 119
Fungus 37, 39

Gale, General Sir Richard 30
Gale, Lady 14, 18, 19, 30, 31, 42
Garlick, Sir John 31, 42
George, Glyn 30, 42, 58
George II, King 22
Gibbons, Grinling 28, 49, 53, 54, 88, 89, 92, 93, 96, 111; carvings 36, 43, 52, 54, 61, 73, 85, 86, 92, 111, 115, 117, 119
Gloucester, HRH The Duke of *99*, 99
Goode, Graham 18
Grace-and-favour 14, 30, 117
graffiti 46, 49
Gray, Ian 30, 42, 54, 58
Great Fountain Garden 61
Guard Chamber 13, *113*, 114

Halahan, Frances 89
Hampton Court Palace 30, 34, 46, 59, 63, 68, 73; aerial view 8; 'Ashes' 84; first-floor plan 27; ground-floor plan 27; history 22; in 1740 *20*; Palace Gardens 43; plan 23; re-opens 35, 43; view 27

handprints 45, 49, *50*, 51, 52, 73, 115
Harrison, Michael 70, 84, 102, 106, 117
Hartley, Richard 86, 89
Henry VIII, King 22, 28, 34, 61, 69, 81, 96
hidden stairs 68
Higgs and Hill 64, 69
Hutton and Rostron 38

Indge, George 42

Jackson, Patricia 52
Jessel, Toby 18
Jones, Inigo 34

Keevil, Jan 115
King's Apartments 27, 34, 65, 68, 85
King's Bedroom 47, 49, *104*, 115, *119*
King Post trusses 77, *77*, 79, 81

Lacey, Charmian 54, *54*
Large Oak Room 81, *81*, *112*, *113*, 116, 117
Law, Ernest 117, 119
Le Sage, John 88, 93
lime trees (wood) 61, 65, 88, 95
Livay, Mrs Ofra 51
Longley, James, and Co. Ltd 64, 69, 70, 71, 73, 76, 81, 84, 99, 102, 103, 106, 117
Luard, David 86, 89, 95

Macdonald, Crawford 116, 119
McNeilage, Torquil 89
Margaret, HRH The Princess 18
Martin, Jo 54, *54*
Mary II, Queen 22, 28, 58, 61
Mayne, Brian 70, 81, 117
mechanical work 60, 84
Medieval Graffiti Society 49
messages, hidden 111, *113*, 114, 117
Millar, Sir Oliver 18
mirrors 45, 52

NADFAS 39

Pain, Colin 54
parapet rebuild 56, 57
photogrammetry 60
Plowden Smith 52
Privy Garden 69, 116
Privy Gates 69, 70, 71
Property Services Agency (PSA) 11, 13, 34, 35, 36, 39, 42, 59, 60, 63, 69, 84, 116, 117

Queen's Gallery 29
Queen Post trusses 73, 76, 77, 77, 81
Quinnell, Richard 77

Raphael Cartoons 13, 119
Rattee and Kett 64, 69
Read, Herbert 89, 93
rectified photographs 60
restoration
  balustrades 69; beam installation 77, *80*, 81; birdcage scaffold 67, 76, 102, 103; brackets, wrought-iron 77, *79*; completion 117; contractor selection 63, 64; costs 35, 60, 69, 111, 117; floors 106; handover documents 116, 117; historical improvements 106, 117; lead roofing 79, 81, 84, 99; panelling 115; planning 60; policy 43; rebuilding 76; roof construction 81; tenders 63, 64, 69; timber purchase 68; topping out 99
Ridout, Brian 38
roof trusses 57, 58, 77, 81
Rosoman, Treve 68
Rydge, Richard 96

salvage *11*, 35, 36, 38, *38*
Salvage Squad 15, 18, 39
sculpture (*Restoration*) 54, *54*, 68
seashells 46, 81, 106, *107*
Second Presence Chamber *14*, *48*, 93
sensors, damp 39, 73
SGB 35
sideboard *112*, 116, 117

Skelmersdale, Lord 63
Small Oak Room 45, 50, 115
South Terrace *13*, 116, 117
State Apartments 13, 15, 27, 34, 43, 52, 84, 102, 103, 117, 119
storms (1987, 1990) 35, 64–5, 99
Stratford Ontario Festival Theatre 63
surveys 60, 61

Talman William 49, 58
Taylor, Keith 58
temporary roof 32, 33, 35, 36, 65, 99, 102
Textile Conservation Studios 18, 111
Think Tank 60
Thorneycroft, John 18, 54
throne canopy 18, *108*, 111
Thurley, Simon 117, 119
Tijou, Jean 28
timber 36, 38, 39, 54, 56, 68, 70, 77, 106
time capsule 117
Tomorrow's World 71, 73
topping out 99
Trinder, Neil 93
trompe-l'oeil painting 49
Turney, Lorna 69

Uppark 85, 99

Vanoli, Dante 84
Verrio, Antonio 28, *104*
Versailles 22
Victoria, Queen 22

West, Juliet 18
William III, King 22, 28, 58, 61
Wolsey Cardinal 22, 81
working party 34, 35, 39, 43, 60, 64, 89, 92
Wren, Sir Christopher 13, 22, 22, 28, 34, 46, 49, 51, 52, 58, 59, 61, 69, 70, 77, 99, 103, 106, 115, 119
Wurtzburg, Sara 68
Wyatt, James 34

York Minster 72, 73